THE DOWNSIDE

A COMEDY IN TWO ACTS

By
RICHARD DRESSER

SAMUEL FRENCH, INC.
45 WEST 25TH STREET   NEW YORK 10010
7623 SUNSET BOULEVARD HOLLYWOOD 90046
LONDON   TORONTO

Copyright ©, 1988, by Richard Dresser

ALL RIGHTS RESERVED

CAUTION: Professionals and amateurs are hereby warned that THE DOWNSIDE is subject to a royalty. It is fully protected under the copyright laws of the United States of America, the British Commonwealth, including Canada, and all other countries of the Copyright Union. All rights, including professional, amateur, motion pictures, recitation, lecturing, public reading, radio broadcasting, television, and the rights of translation into foreign languages are strictly reserved. In its present form the play is dedicated to the reading public only.

THE DOWNSIDE may be given stage presentation by amateurs in theatres seating less than 500 upon payment of a royalty of Fifty Dollars for the first performance, and Thirty-five Dollars for each additional performance. PLEASE NOTE: for amateur productions in theatres seating over 500, write for special royalty quotation, giving details as to ticket price, number of performances and exact number of seats in your theatre. Royalties are payable one week before the opening performance of the play, to Samuel French, Inc., at 45 W. 25th St., New York, NY 10010; or at 7623 Sunset Blvd., Hollywood, CA 90046, or to Samuel French (Canada), Ltd., 80 Richmond St. East, Toronto, Ontario, Canada M5C 1P1.

Royalty of the required amount must be paid whether the play is presented for charity or gain and whether or not admission is charged.

Stock royalty quoted on application to Samuel French, Inc.

For all other rights than those stipulated above, apply to Jeannine Edmunds, Artists Agency, 230 W. 55th St. #29-D, New York, NY 10019.

Particular emphasis is laid on the question of amateur or professional readings, permission and terms for which must be secured in writing from Samuel French, Inc.

Copying from this book in whole or in part is strictly forbidden by law, and the right of performance is not transferable.

Whenever the play is produced the following notice must appear on all programs, printing and advertising for the play: "Produced by special arrangement with Samuel French, Inc."

Due authorship credit must be given on all programs, printing and advertising for the play.

Anyone presenting the play shall not commit or authorize any act or omission by which the copyright of the play or the right to copyright same may be impaired.

No changes shall be made in the play for the purpose of your production unless authorized in writing.

The publication of this play does not imply that it is necessarily available for performance by amateurs or professionals. Amateurs and professionals considering a production are strongly advised in their own interests to apply to Samuel French, Inc., for consent before starting rehearsals, advertising, or booking a theatre or hall.

No part of this book may be reproduced, stored in a retrieval system, or transmitted in any form, by any means, including mechanical, electronic, photocopying, recording, or otherwise, without the prior written permission of the publisher.

ISBN 0 573 67047 1   Printed in U.S.A.

IMPORTANT BILLING AND CREDIT REQUIREMENTS

All producers of THE DOWNSIDE *must* give credit to the Author of the Play in all programs distributed in connection with performances of the Play and in all instances in which the title of the Play appears for purposes of advertising, publicizing or otherwise exploiting the Play and/or a production. The name of the Author *must* also appear on a separate line, in which no other name appears, immediately following the title, and *must* appear in size of type not less than fifty percent the size of the title type.

POWERHOUSE THEATER AT VASSAR

BETH FARGIS-LANCASTER, *Producing Director*
EVERT SPRINCHORN, *Educational Director*

presents the

NEW YORK STAGE AND FILM COMPANY

Producing Directors

MARK LINN-BAKER MAX MAYER LESLIE URDANG

production of

THE DOWNSIDE
by RICHARD DRESSER
Directed by KENNETH FRANKEL

Sets by
James D. Sandefur

Costumes by
Jess Goldstein

Lights by
Don Holder

Sound by
Brent Evans

Production Stage Manager
William H. Lang

Stage Manager
Heidi M. Schultz

Production Manager
Alfred Miller

THE DOWNSIDE
CAST
(in order of appearance)

Roxanne .... DANA DELANY*
Diane .... GAIL DARTEZ*
Jeff .... RANDALL MELL*
Ben .... DENNIS BOUTSIKARIS*
Alan .... EDDIE JONES*
Carl .... PETER CROMBIE*
Stan .... MICHAEL ALBERT MANTEL*
Gary .... PAUL GUILFOYLE*
Dave .... DANIEL DE RAEY*
*AEA member

THE DOWNSIDE PRODUCTION STAFF

Technical Director .... JON CARLSON
Costume Shop Manager .... SUSAN WOOD
Scenic Artist .... JOHN SHIMROCK
Property Master .... BETH DOYLE
Master Carpenter .... ALVIN SCHUH
Assistant Stage Manager ... RHONDA L. ANDERSON

LONG WHARF THEATRE

Presents

The DOWNSIDE

a new American play
by Richard Dresser
directed by Kenneth Frankel

Set Design by
LOREN SHERMAN

Costume Design by
JESS GOLDSTEIN

Lighting Design by
JUDY RASMUSON

Production Stage Manager
ROBIN KEVRICK

October 16-November 29, 1987

Arvin Brown, Artistic Director
M. Edgar Rosenblum, Executive Director

THE CAST *(in order of appearance)*

Roxanne	LISA PELIKAN
Diane	J. SMITH-CAMERON
Jeff	BRUCE DAVISON
Ben	MARK BLUM
Alan	EDDIE JONES
Carl	KEVIN O'ROURKE
Stan	PETER ZAPP
Gary	PAUL GUILFOYLE
Dave	DANIEL DE RAEY

The action of the play takes place in the marketing department of Mark & Maxwell, a pharmaceutical company in New Jersey.

ACT I *Scene 1 – Monday morning, early December*
  Scene 2 – Friday morning of the following week
  Scene 3 – Monday morning after Christmas

ACT II *Scene 1 – The next morning*
  Scene 2 – Monday morning, two weeks later
  Scene 3 – The next morning

SETTING

The marketing department of Mark & Maxwell, a pharmaceutical company in New Jersey.

It's a modern, suburban complex. Outside there are fountains, sculptures, and manicured grounds. Inside, there's a shiny, efficient sterility. Doors slide silently open when approached, telephones ring discreetly, and there's an aura of extreme control.

What we see are the sleek, modern offices of the marketing department. We also see the reception area and the conference room, which has a long table.

The action takes place over a month in December and January.

CHARACTERS

BEN	late thirties
JEFF	late thirties
DIANE	mid-thirties
ROXANNE	mid-twenties
CARL	forties
ALAN	early sixties
STAN	thirty
GARY	late thirties

THE DOWNSIDE

ACT I

Scene 1

SCENE: Monday morning, early December. LIGHTS up on the reception area. We see ROXANNE's desk, a leather sofa, and a coffee machine.

AT RISE: ROXANNE, the receptionist, is on the phone. She's in her mid-twenties and very stylishly dressed. DIANE, one of the marketing directors, Enters from outside. She's in her mid-thirties and is wearing a winter coat over a conservative business suit.

ROXANNE. *(on phone)* Yes ... yes .... right. Fine. I'll tell him. I know. Yes, you did mention that. Goodbye. *(She hangs up the phone.)*

DIANE. So how was it?

ROXANNE. What?

DIANE. You know, your date. With the investment banker—

ROXANNE. Oh, Todd.

DIANE. I thought you were dying to go out with this guy.

ROXANNE. It was great.

DIANE. Really great? Or just, you know...I mean you said he was really gorgeous.

ROXANNE. What happened was we went to a super party and I met this guy Mark, who is incredibly rich, and we kind of hit it off so went back to his place—

DIANE. Mark's place?

ROXANNE. No, Todd's—

DIANE. You went to Todd's place with Mark?

ROXANNE. And Todd—

DIANE. The three of you?

ROXANNE. It was really fun.

DIANE. Todd didn't mind?

ROXANNE. At first he was a real prude, I mean, he *is* a banker, like he would leave the room when I was with Mark and he made Mark leave the room when I was with him, but then Mark got out this coke and Todd got into it and didn't even make me leave the room when he was with Mark. *(She picks up the coffee pot.)* Coffee?

DIANE. Thanks.

ROXANNE. *(Pours coffee for DIANE.)* So Todd had to work in the morning and he wasn't crazy about leaving me and Mark in his apartment but we hung out there anyway. Mark wanted me to tie him up, but that was the one thing I wouldn't do because I feel like Todd and I could have a really long-term relationship if we're willing to work at it.

DIANE. Sounds like it.

ROXANNE. So what did you do this week-end?

DIANE. Not much. I had a lot of work to do.

ROXANNE. Did you see Bob?

DIANE. No...he was pretty busy. You know, his first

week-end back in almost eight months. We talked on the phone.

ROXANNE. You're still engaged, aren't you?
DIANE. *(flashing her ring)* Going on three years now.

(DIANE goes to her office. JEFF, another marketing director, Enters from outside. He's in his late thirties.)

JEFF. Hi beautiful. How was your week-end?
ROXANNE. None of your business.
JEFF. That good? *(He gets coffee.)*
ROXANNE. You had a call from a Mr. Chevette.
JEFF. Yeah? The old man here?
ROXANNE. In his office. He keeps getting here earlier and earlier—
JEFF. Somebody's gotta teach him how to tell time.

(JEFF starts for his office as BEN, another marketing director, Enters from outside. He has a bandage over his eye. He's unshaven and hung-over.)

JEFF. Morning, Ben.
BEN. What's that s'posed to mean?
ROXANNE. Hey, are you okay?
BEN. Fine. Thanks.
ROXANNE. You want some coffee, Ben?
BEN. Nah, it'll just keep me awake all day—
JEFF. We got a meeting, remember?
BEN. Forget it. I'm crashing.
ROXANNE. Dave's going to be there.
JEFF. Really? In person?

BEN. What's happening?

ROXANNE. You think I know?

JEFF. She knows everything.

BEN. I'll be in the conference room. If I go to my office I'll just sleep. *(BEN starts for the conference room. JEFF follows. ROXANNE starts to work.)*

(CROSS FADE to the conference room. BEN throws his briefcase and coat on the conference table.)

BEN. Those fucking Giants—

JEFF. What Giants?

BEN. Man, I could have kicked that field goal from my living room. Thirty yards out—did you see it? It looked like the Elephant Man out there.

JEFF. I thought you weren't going to bet anymore—

BEN. Jeff, it was in my pocket, the money was in my pocket 'til that son of a bitch blew it. It was a smart bet, a courageous bet—

JEFF. How much did you lose?

BEN. For Chrissakes, Jeffrey, it's Monday morning, I feel like shit. My wife—

JEFF. She hit you?

BEN. Great. Why don't you talk a little louder?

JEFF. I'm your friend, and when you come in with this bandage I have to ask you why.

BEN. It's a financial matter.

JEFF. Your bookie hit you?

BEN. What, are you crazy? Jack is my friend. I've know him since high school. *(beat)* He called me after the game, said he wanted to meet me at Chico's, you know that Mexican joint in the center of town—

JEFF. The food really sucks there. You want good Mexican you gotta go into the city—

BEN. Meanwhile, I've been having this fight with my wife that has been going on for, like, days. I was just getting it together to see her point of view when that little Hungarian dick-head misses the field goal, and, you know, I expressed my feelings for a while, like, remember that compact disk player she just bought? Gone. The TV? Gone. Half the furniture? Gone—

JEFF. Great. Don't keep those feelings bottled up inside, Ben—

BEN. So the phone rings, it's Jack, my wife doesn't understand why I have to go, big fight, I go. Jack's there in front of Chico's in a big Buick with this other guy. I walk over, chat with Jack, he mentions that, like, my payments have not been all that punctual, and I'm saying, yeah, Jack, but even American Express gives you a little time. Then his friend gets out and walks over and I actually stick out my hand to introduce myself and the son of a bitch clocks me. Just like that. I look at Jack and I feel the blood running down my face and he's just staring at me. I say, Jack, what the fuck. And he says, keep in touch, buddy. And they drive off. I'm standing there in the center of town on a Sunday afternoon bleeding. I went to high school with Jack.

JEFF. What did you do?

BEN. I go back home, but she's got all the doors locked and she won't let me in. I look in the window and the whole house is busted up and she's just sitting on the sofa, staring straight ahead. It was like looking at my own death scene. *(beat)* So how was your week-end?

JEFF. Did you try to talk to her?

BEN. Talk? We don't have that kind of relationship.

JEFF. You better get your shit together, buddy.

BEN. You mean you did something different?

JEFF. We spent the whole week-end together. As a family. Cross-country skiing, watched a coupla flicks on the VCR. Every night, before I turn in I go into my daughter's room. I watch her sleeping. It's religious, it's like what you're s'posed to feel in church.

(ROXANNE Enters with legal pads.)

JEFF. How come you always look so nice?

ROXANNE. It's all for you, Jeff, all for you.

JEFF. No, seriously, most women have some days they look good, some days not so good, but you look terrific all the time.

ROXANNE. Jeff? It's Monday morning. Give it a rest.
(ROXANNE leaves.)

JEFF. She hates me.

BEN. She doesn't hate you.

JEFF. I would give ten years off my life to get it on with her. Ten years, easy.

BEN. Me too.

JEFF. You like her?

BEN. Enough to give ten years of your life—

JEFF. I would even give, maybe a year off my life just to see her with no clothes on...or, say, all my vacations for three years—

BEN. You're a hopeless romantic, Jeff—

JEFF. Honest to God, I get this feeling from her—

BEN. Like the feeling you're s'posed to have in church?

JEFF. The one time she agreed to go out to lunch with me, I figure, a long lunch...you know what we did?

BEN. What?

JEFF. We ate lunch.

BEN. No kidding?

JEFF. Absolutely. Very weird chick.

BEN. I don't get this, Jeff. You have this wonderful, loving family that just walked out of a Hallmark card, and you are desperate for women. And me, I am utterly faithful to a bad marriage.

JEFF. Maybe you oughta move on her.

BEN. Me?

JEFF. I could definitely see the two of you together. I see you at some cozy little restaurant with candles and annoying music and minority people bringing you food and she's whispering in your ear about wanting to go home. Now you're in bed, her bed, and it's a water bed. You know, Ben, the first time I laid eyes on her I knew she had a water bed, it's written all over her—

BEN. You can see all this because she's weird? What does that make me?

JEFF. Miserable. Beat up by bookies. Trapped in this horrible thing—

BEN. You mean my marriage—

JEFF. And you better stop and smell the flowers because life is too short—

BEN. Not my life. My life is definitely not too short.

JEFF. That's just what I'm saying. You've got to take some kind of control over your life before it runs away with you.

(DIANE Enters.)

JEFF. Hello, Diane.
DIANE. Hi Jeff. Hey, are you okay, Ben?
BEN. Oh, yeah.
DIANE. What happened?
BEN. Oh, I was working in the basement. This thing fell on me. How was your week-end?
DIANE. Oh, very nice. Busy. How 'bout you?
BEN. Pretty good. Watched a little football on the tube. It was fun.
JEFF. You know Dave's coming to the meeting?
DIANE. Dave? What's happening?
BEN. No one knows.

(ALAN Enters. He's the head of marketing, in his sixties. Everybody says good morning.)

ALAN. Everyone have a good week-end? *(mumbled assents)* Good. Because you won't be seeing much of your loved ones for a while.
JEFF. What's going on?
ALAN. I'll let Dave tell you—
DIANE. He's really going to be here?
ALAN. At the last minute he had to fly to L.A. Board meeting. So we'll put him on the box.

ACT I THE DOWNSIDE 17

(ROXANNE Enters.)

ALAN. Where's Carl? He's back from vacation today, right?
DIANE. He's supposed to be.
ALAN. If anyone's missing it might as well be Carl. Ben, move down one. Roxanne, put Dave at the head of the table. *(ROXANNE puts a speaker box at the head of the table.)*
ALAN. Have we got him?
ROXANNE. Central switchboard has him. I'll put him through whenever you're ready.
ALAN. We're ready.
ROXANNE. *(To the speaker box.)* Mr. Godfrey?

(DAVE'S voice is heard on the speaker. He sounds calm, brisk, always in control, like an airplane pilot.)

DAVE. *(off)* Morning, everybody. *(mumbled "good mornings")*
ALAN. David! How's the weather out there, buddy? *(ROXANNE Exits to reception.)*
DAVE. *(off)* I'm still here at the airport, Alan. This new Executive Telephone is fantastic, you can take it anywhere.

(We hear AIRPORT SOUNDS in the background.)

DAVE. They're calling my flight, so I'll make this quick. We've made the decision to launch Maxolan-3000 in January. I know that's quite a change from what we first announced—

JEFF. You mean we're pushing it back six months?

DAVE. *(off)* That you, Jeff?

JEFF. Yes, Dave.

DAVE. *(off)* Jeff, I'm talking about this coming January. We're moving it up six months—

JEFF. You mean we're launching it next month?

DAVE. *(off)* We've got an opportunity here to really run with the ball. Obviously, it means some deadline pressures for your squad, but I'm confident that you can rise to the occasion. The exact launch date is the tenth, and I'm looking for the kind of push that will put us ahead of the pack right away. The word on Lovelle is they won't be ready to go until June at the earliest, so we should have the field to ourselves for a couple of months if we're willing to roll up our sleeves and go to work. Alan's got the specifics of it, but I just wanted to wish you all the best and tell you how much the company is counting on you. I think the more you acquaint yourselves with the product, the more excited you'll be about its potential. Any questions?

BEN. Can we get FDA approval by January?

DAVE. *(off)* That ball's in my court, people. I'll get us the approval.

DIANE. Will we have the usual problems? What about production?

DAVE. *(off)* I'm giving you my personal assurance there will be no back orders. Manufacturing is backing us up one hundred percent. I don't need to tell you what a difficult year this has been for all of us with the lay-offs. Third quarter earnings were not encouraging, and we're looking at more changes at every level of the organization. How you perform over the next month could well determine where you are in January. Good luck.

ALAN. Thanks, Dave. I know my team is as thrilled as I am by this challenge. You can count on the best launch we've ever done.

DAVE. *(off)* There's my flight...I'll be checking in from L.A.

ALAN. Have a terrific trip, Dave. We're off and running.

(DIAL TONE from the speaker. ALAN lights a cigarette. His hands are trembling.)

ALAN. Mother of God.

BEN. Does anyone have any aspirin? *(DIANE gives him some. They all turn on ALAN.)*

JEFF. How can we get this together by the tenth?

ALAN. Into the Valley of Death rode the four hundred...

DIANE. What's this about more personnel changes at every level of the corporation?

JEFF. They've already had their blood-bath. Now they want us in here day and night...

ALAN. He's after me. He's trying to get me out.

JEFF. Hey, Alan. It's okay. We can do it—

DIANE. We're not going to let you down.

(ROXANNE Enters.)

ROXANNE. Alan? Mr. Oates is here to see you. Says he had an appointment?

ALAN. Oh, God, yes. I forgot. I'll see him in a few minutes. And bring him in here. *(ROXANNE Exits.)*

JEFF. What's the hurry? Who is this guy?

ALAN. Dave's pushing him at me.

JEFF. For what?

ALAN. Someone else has to go. By Christmas. Dave's leaving it up to me.

BEN. What about the hiring freeze? *(ALAN leaves.)* If I wanted to be this miserable I could stay home.

DIANE. Do you think they're really after Alan?

JEFF. I think Carl is the one who's gone.

DIANE. Carl?

BEN. He's history, definitely.

JEFF. If they're getting rid of dead wood—

BEN. They should have iced him first. You think of all the people they fired this year, I mean how did Carl survive?

DIANE. I can't stand the atmosphere around here. It's like the French Revolution—

JEFF. I'll miss Carl, no question. He was the kind of guy who made everyone else look good—

BEN. We need more Carls around here. This rising level of competence is starting to scare me—

DIANE. He had his good points.

BEN. Yeah? Name one.

(CARL Enters. He's in his forties, wearing a parka.)

DIANE. Carl!

CARL. The plane was late. I came straight here and saw this memo for the meeting—

JEFF. Hey, buddy. Good to see you.

BEN. So how was the vacation, pal? We missed you.

CARL. Three words. Un-be-lievable. A real eye-opener—

DIANE. You went to Alaska?

CARL. What they do, is, they drop you out of a plane with nothing but a Swiss Army knife and your native intellect—

BEN. —so all you had was the knife?

CARL. —and you learn what it takes to survive. Almost everyone in our group made it. It takes you right out to the very edge of your existence and you discover what is truly important—

JEFF. What does it cost?

CARL. The whole package — survivalist training, the works — is three grand.

BEN. Three grand to get pushed out of a plane? Where do I sign up?

CARL. They got another one, they'll drop you in this place in South America where there are cannibals. Actual cannibals. Man, I'm there.

BEN. You don't need to leave here to find cannibals, Carl. You missed the meeting.

CARL. What's happening?

DIANE. Maxolan-3000 is coming, Carl.

JEFF. In January.

CARL. They pushed it back again?

BEN. This January, Carl.

CARL. That soon? I guess it will be a busy month. *(beat)* Well, I'll see you later. *(CARL Exits.)*

DIANE. How come he never gets upset?

JEFF. Because he never understands the situation.

BEN. Somebody oughta clue him in so he can make plans. It's pretty cold to put someone out on the street at Christmas.

DIANE. I think we should at least have a going away party for him. How long has he been here? Seven years?

JEFF. I'll talk to Roxie.

DIANE. I'll start digging up everything we've got on Maxolan. *(DIANE leaves.)*

JEFF. I could give a rusty fuck about Carl. It's Alan—

BEN. The man is hurting.

JEFF. The man is not going to make it.

BEN. You think they'll bring in someone new?

JEFF. They can't have someone learning the ropes with a deadline like this. I think they'll promote someone who's already here.

BEN. There aren't too many of us left.

JEFF. That's what I'm thinking. I'll catch you later.

(CROSS FADE to reception area. ROXANNE is working at a computer. JEFF Enters.)

JEFF. Roxie? Can I talk to you?

ROXANNE. It sounds that way.

JEFF. I mean in private.

ROXANNE. How private?

JEFF. You, me, a pitcher of margaritas—

ROXANNE. Jeff, I have a lot of work, okay?

JEFF. I was wondering if you could organize a party for Carl.

ROXANNE. Carl?

JEFF. He's dead in the water.

ROXANNE. When?

JEFF. They'll remove the body by the holidays.

ROXANNE. That's not a lot of time. I've got my hands full—

JEFF. Okay, we'll skip it. Let him just walk out with nothing.

ROXANNE. I guess we could combine it with the Christmas party.

JEFF. That's fine. I just hope Carl doesn't feel upstaged by Jesus.

(CROSS FADE to the conference room. ALAN is talking to STAN OATES, who's about thirty, a little hesitant, wearing clothes that don't quite make it.)

ALAN. Personnel sent your resume down. You certainly have a...diverse background.

STAN. Thank you.

ALAN. Let's see, you've had, what, about twelve different jobs since you got out of business school?

STAN. Right.

ALAN. You like to move around. San Jose, Atlanta, Houston, Detroit—

STAN. It's been interesting to see different parts of our country.

ALAN. And it's not as though you've limited yourself to one business. Electronics, fast-food, publishing, plastics—

STAN. I've had a lot of different opportunities.

ALAN. That's wonderful. Must be exciting, moving from one job to the next every six months.

STAN. I feel that it adds up to excellent experience.

ALAN. I certainly don't doubt your abilities, Stan, but I do wonder how long you might want to stay with us. Maybe this is just a quirk of our organization, but we usually like to hire people for more than a few months.

STAN. I'm excited about your company, Mr. Baylor. I look forward to years of quality service.

ALAN. I guess you know this is a somewhat unusual situation. We often use the job interview as a factor in our hiring decision, but you have a recommendation here that virtually obliges me to hire you. Were you aware of that?

STAN. I know people have always been happy with my work.

ALAN. Dave Godfrey's letter is a little more definite than that. So this is really just a formality, assuming you want the job.

STAN. I wouldn't be here if I didn't want the job.

ALAN. You'll be coming in at a very difficult time. We have a deadline crunch on a new product. Plus, quite frankly, the whole corporation has been engaged in a reduction and restructuring of all personnel, which means you might not last very long. Even with this letter.

STAN. I only want a fair chance.

ALAN. I guess what I'm really telling you, Stan, is that I have to hire you. But you don't have to accept the job. In my estimation, if you take a job at this company at this time then you are hurling yourself naked into a pit of poisonous snakes.

STAN. I welcome the challenge, Mr. Baylor. *(ALAN stares at STAN, then tries to call ROXANNE on the intercom.)*

ALAN. Roxanne? Roxanne? Goddammit *(He gives up on the intercom and yells to her.)* Roxanne! *(to STAN:)* New phone system.

(ROXANNE Enters.)

ROXANNE. Something wrong with the intercom?
ALAN. I can't work this goddam thing.
ROXANNE. For the intercom you press this button. Or you can just leave the switch here on "voice."
ALAN. Okay, leave it on "voice."
ROXANNE. You remember how that works?
ALAN. Pretty much. I'll figure it out...
ROXANNE. It means that when you want to reach anyone in the office, you just say their full name. It's encoded with your voice print—
ALAN. Right, right. So I say...Jeffrey Blaine.

(LIGHTS UP on JEFF'S office. His PHONE RINGS. He answers it.)

JEFF. Hello?
ROXANNE. And it's like the intercom, you don't even need to pick up—
JEFF. Hello?
ALAN. Hi, Jeff. I'm sending someone over to your office, okay?

JEFF. Fine, Alan.

(LIGHTS DOWN on JEFF'S office.)

ALAN. That's incredible. It's like having a phone inside my head—
ROXANNE. Did you want me for anything else, Alan?
ALAN. This is Stanley Oates—
ROXANNE. We met.
ALAN. Would you get his paperwork in order and take him to Jeff's office so he can get oriented? He'll be joining us immediately. *(ALAN and STAN shake hands.)* You're coming in at a tough time, Stan. We'll try to get you up to speed in a hurry.
STAN. I appreciate it, Mr. Baylor.

(CROSS FADE to JEFF'S office. JEFF is using a dictaphone.)

JEFF. Relax to the max with Maxolan-3000...over fours years use in Europe...unquestioned safety record ...now available for the first time...

(ROXANNE Enters with STAN.)

ROXANNE. Sorry to bother you. Jeff, this is Stan Oates...Jeff Blaine.
JEFF. Hi, Stan.
STAN. Hello.
ROXANNE. Alan wants you to get Stan oriented. He works here now. *(ROXANNE Exits.)*
JEFF. Shit. *(beat)* Sorry, Stan. I'm just a little under the

gun right now.

STAN. That's okay. I can wait outside—

JEFF. No, as long as you're on board, you'll have to plunge in with the rest of us. See, we have a product called Maxolan-3000. It's been sold in Europe for a while and we've closed the deal to market it in this country. It's an anti-hypertensive, you know, for the treatment of stress. We have word that FDA is giving fast approval because they aren't happy with the drugs that are out there on the market now. What we have is a slight reformulation of the European product which expedites the manufacturing process and we're busting our asses to get it on the market by January tenth. We'll beat the closest competition by a couple of months. We want sales to give it highest priority—your background is in the pharmaceutical business, I assume?

STAN. Actually not.

JEFF. What is your background?

STAN. It's, uh, pretty diverse. Electronics—

JEFF. Electronics?

STAN. Other areas as well.

JEFF. So you've never marketed pharmaceuticals?

STAN. Not until now. But I welcome the challenge—

JEFF. They're replacing Carl with someone with no background? Jesus Christ. I wonder if they'll give us blindfolds...

(CARL Enters.)

CARL. You got a minute, Jeff?

JEFF. Any time, Carl. This is Stan...Stan, Carl. *(They shake hands.)*

CARL. *(to JEFF.)* I've got a problem—

JEFF. I know you do.

CARL. I can't get enough guys together for the basketball team this winter. When Lloyd and Phil got fired that was it for our front line, so I was wondering if maybe you could step in—

JEFF. I don't think you oughta be worrying about that, Carl.

CARL. Why not?

JEFF. Let's just say if I were you I wouldn't be doing anything extra for the company.

CARL. I've got the time.

JEFF. More than you think.

STAN. I'll play ball, Carl.

CARL. It's for employees only.

JEFF. Stan was just hired.

CARL. Really? That's great. You're a guard?

STAN. Haven't played much since high school but I'd love to get out there.

JEFF. I'm gonna get some coffee. *(JEFF Exits.)*

CARL. I've been on vacation. Is this your first day?

STAN. Just got here.

CARL. Is somebody leaving? Because we've had a hiring freeze.

STAN. They didn't tell me.

CARL. Welcome aboard.

STAN. Thanks. I welcome the challenge.

CARL. Come on. I'll show you around.

(BLACKOUT)

END OF ACT I, SCENE 1

Scene 2

Friday, the following week. LIGHTS UP on the reception area. ROXANNE is putting up Christmas decorations. DIANE Enters from outside.

DIANE. God, it's miserable out there.

ROXANNE. It's s'posed to snow all day.

DIANE. I'm exhausted. I didn't sleep all night.

ROXANNE. Bob?

DIANE. Work. I feel like I didn't even leave this place.

ROXANNE. You saw Bob, didn't you?

DIANE. We talked. He's trying to decide between getting married or taking another year of training in Tibet.

ROXANNE. What exactly is he training for?

DIANE. Oh, you know, he does these training sessions with executives. To open up their creativity—

ROXANNE. So he's training to do more training—

DIANE. He figures one solid year of meditation, he can make it through about four levels which translates into maybe another forty grand a year when he comes back—

ROXANNE. Not bad.

DIANE. I don't know. The first couple of years we were engaged it was pretty exciting, but now it's just something in the future that's going to happen—

ROXANNE. Like death.

DIANE. Exactly. *(beat)* So, did you see Todd last night?

ROXANNE. Mark. Todd the night before.

DIANE. You like Mark?

ROXANNE. He can go all night. We started before the six o'clock news and ended up missing Johnny's monologue. *(beat)* He even wants me to move in with him.

DIANE. Boy, that's fast. Are you going to?

ROXANNE. I don't know. He lives at home.

DIANE. With his parents?

ROXANNE. No, he threw them out last summer. He just got fed up with their routines so he made them leave.

DIANE. He threw his parents out of their own house? Where did they go?

ROXANNE. They just took off in their camper. He told them not to even think about coming back 'til they get their shit together. He's kind of spoiled.

DIANE. God.

ROXANNE. The house is really great, it's got a pool and everything. I might actually move in if he'll let me still go out with Todd. *(beat)* If you want a break later I'll be setting up for the party.

DIANE. I'll try. I don't have much free time these days.

(CROSS FADE to Ben's office. BEN is gargling at his desk. JEFF Enters.)

JEFF. How 'bout those Giants, huh?

BEN. Don't mention those bums to me.

JEFF. For Chrissakes, they finally won.

BEN. Yeah, they had to pick last night to win. After I finally got smart and bet against 'em.

JEFF. You bet against them?

BEN. I was in this bar screaming, "Choke! Choke!" I didn't make a lot of friends last night.

JEFF. Did Jack come after you for the money?

BEN. I don't know.

JEFF. You don't know?

BEN. I wasn't home.

JEFF. Where were you?

BEN. Jeff, I'm spending a lot of time in my office these days.

JEFF. I know. It smells like a locker room in here—

BEN. A lot of time. Like all my time.

JEFF. You're living here?

BEN. I haven't been home in four days. We figured we could recapture the magic in our relationship if we never saw each other again.

JEFF. I'm really sorry. You can stay at my house—

BEN. No, this is fine. It's the only way I can get to work on time.

JEFF. Is there anything I can do?

BEN. What, you don't think I'll be happy here?

JEFF. You're probably the only one that'll make it home safely after the party.

BEN. Jesus Christ. The party.

JEFF. It's Carl's last day. The old man said he'd make the change by the holidays.

BEN. Poor bastard.

JEFF. He and Stan have gotten really tight. Stan

actually listens to what Carl says.

BEN. That's insane.

JEFF. That fucking Stan is driving me nuts. I have to hide to get away from him. I finally gave him an assignment so he'd leave me alone.

BEN. How come you're in charge of Stan?

JEFF. Maybe the old man is getting back at me for something—

BEN. Or maybe he's giving you more responsibility so you can take over for him.

JEFF. You think so?

BEN. I got a feeling one of us is headed for the big office.

(CARL and STAN Enter.)

CARL. Hey, Ben. You want a ride or shall we just meet at the gym?

BEN. What are you talking about?

CARL. You don't remember? You sounded half asleep.

BEN. When?

CARL. When I called your house this morning. I asked if you wanted to play basketball tomorrow afternoon since Stan had to cancel and you said fine and hung up.

JEFF. You must have dialed a wrong number, Carl.

CARL. No way. I've got your number programmed into my phone. I dialed your house this morning and this voice said—

BEN. Okay, Carl. I'll play basketball.

ACT I   THE DOWNSIDE   33

CARL. Great. Two o'clock, tomorrow afternoon. Hey, you see that Giants game? Un-be-lievable! *(CARL and STAN Exit.)*

BEN. Well, she didn't waste any time, did she?

JEFF. You don't know—

BEN. Believe me, I know.

JEFF. Fucking Carl. Dead and still walking around.

(CROSS FADE to the conference room, which is decorated for the Christmas party. CARL and STAN are at the table. BEN and JEFF Enter.)

JEFF. Where's the old man?

CARL. Nobody's seen him.

STAN. Jeff? Have you got time to look at my outline for the launch?

JEFF. Later, Stan. Can I give you some friendly advice?

STAN. Of course, Jeff.

JEFF. You're never going to go anywhere in this corporation dressed like that. You oughta save your pennies and buy a suit. I look at that sportcoat and I think, "There's a guy on his way to see female mud-wrestling—"

BEN. Take it easy, Jeff.

JEFF. I'm saying this 'cause I care. Stan understands that, right, Stan?

STAN. Sure. Thanks, Jeff.

JEFF. Any time.

(DIANE Enters.)

DIANE. Does he want specific stuff? Because I'm in the middle of everything and I'd rather keep it general—

BEN. You seen Alan?

DIANE. Where is he?

(ROXANNE Enters with legal pads.)

JEFF. Hey, Roxie. Is Alan here?

ROXANNE. He hasn't showed up.

JEFF. Maybe you oughta call his house—

ROXANNE. I've been calling his house. No answer. Dave is on the line. *(beat)* Shall I put him on?

JEFF. What the hell.

ROXANNE. *(to the speaker:)* Mr. Godfrey? Are you there?

DAVE. Morning, everybody. *(mumbled good mornings)*

JEFF. How's the weather out there, Dave?

DAVE. It's terrific, Alan—

JEFF. Jeff.

DAVE. Sorry, Jeff. Alan, I've only got a minute here, I'm at a breakfast meeting and then I'm getting on a plane. They've got some kind of live entertainment planned, you know L.A.—

JEFF. Alan isn't here, Dave.

DAVE. Where is he?

JEFF. He's out sick.

DAVE. Roxanne, you can put me through to his house. I just wanted all of you to know I'm with you every step of the way—

(MUSIC from the speaker.)

DAVE. The, uh, entertainment is starting here. I'm going to have to sign off, but I think you should know how much this launch means to the future of the company. I've been in meetings all week, and I won't pull any punches...

(ALAN Enters.)

DAVE. The bottom line is, we either make a go of it with Maxolan-3000 or we—

ALAN. That's not the bottom line. The bottom line is we die and become nothingness for all eternity. That's the bottom line.

DAVE. Is that you, Alan?

ALAN. Oh, Dave has joined us. Hello, Dave. You're looking well today. Isn't Dave looking well? Sorry I'm late. I've had such trouble sleeping. Last night I got up and looked out the window and there in the middle of my yard in the moonlight was a man. He was staring at the house, three o'clock in the morning. He had a suit on. I put on my bathrobe and went out on the step and by God I recognized him. It was Nixon. I didn't know whether to invite him in or what, I mean what the hell do you do with Richard Nixon? So I just stared at Nixon and Nixon stared at me and then I went back inside and slept like a baby. That's why I'm a little late, Dave.

DAVE. What the hell is going on there?

ALAN. In the morning he was gone. Nixon was gone. But he left his footprints, like a yeti. *(A beat, then they try to cover.)*

JEFF. Dave, we've made real progress in the past week.

We feel that we haven't exploited the video potential of our operation to its fullest extent. Alan is meeting with an outside media consultant today—

BEN. And Dave, I have to say, the more we discover about Maxolan the more enthusiastic we are about its possibilities. We've come up with several—

JEFF. —exciting—

DIANE. —approaches. We really feel good about the product and now our job is to get sales behind it. I'm working on learning systems that will take a step by step approach to Maxolan—

CARL. And Dave? I think launch strategy is key.

(They all stare at CARL. LAUGHTER in the background on the speaker.)

DAVE. Look, I've got to go, they're bringing out some damn comics. I'm catching a flight out of here right after breakfast so I'll see you soon. And for Chrissakes, Alan, get some sleep, would you?

ALAN. I'll do that, Dave. Did I tell you you're looking terrific today?

DAVE. When you're ready to talk, we've got things to talk about, Alan.

(DIAL TONE. ALAN turns off the speaker. Silence. ROXANNE Exits.)

JEFF. Alan? Is something wrong?

ALAN. Nothing's wrong.

BEN. Why don't the rest of your clear out, okay?

ACT I   **THE DOWNSIDE**   37

(CARL, STAN, and DIANE leave.) You want some coffee, Alan?

ALAN. Yeah, fine. Coffee.

ROXANNE. *(on intercom)* Ben? You have a call from a Mr. Vito?

BEN. I'll call him back, okay?

ROXANNE. He sounds very upset.

BEN. I'll take it in my office. *(BEN Exits.)*

JEFF. You feel better? Huh? You didn't take a drink today, did you?

ALAN. In the fucking morning?

JEFF. Maybe you better go home—

ALAN. I'm fine. I'm here. I want to stay.

JEFF. You feel well enough to meet with Gary Chevette?

ALAN. Who?

JEFF. The media consultant. Remember? The guy I went to college with?

ALAN. I'll talk to him.

JEFF. Because I think it could make a real difference—

ALAN. I'll talk to him, Jeff.

(BEN Enters with coffee for ALAN.)

JEFF. How's Mr. Vito?

BEN. I still got both my knee-caps, don't I?

JEFF. This is Jack's partner?

BEN. I told him never to call this office again. Then I hung up on him. Dumb son of a bitch.

ALAN. Who's this?

JEFF. Friend of Ben's.

BEN. You okay, Alan?

ALAN. Yeah, yeah, I'm fine. *(beat)* It's just...if those bastards fire me it will kill me. Forty years I've been here, I've seen'em come and go, for Chrissakes, I remember when Dave came in, a nervous kid just out of school. When my wife was sick I was still here every night 'til eight o'clock and first one here in the morning. In all those years I took one personal day and that was for the funeral. I think of staying in that house by myself every day—

JEFF. Alan. Nobody's going to fire you.

ALAN. I get so goddam lonely. I need a woman. You know where I can find a woman?

JEFF. What are we talking about, Alan? A prostitute or a relationship?

ALAN. It's only six months since my wife is buried, Jeff, you think I would tarnish her memory with a relationship?

JEFF. Well, if it's prostitutes Ben probably knows better than me—

BEN. Fuck you.

JEFF. —but I hear the Holiday Inn near the airport, the lounge...you drop by after eleven they'll set you up good.

BEN. Yeah?

ALAN. Thanks, Jeff. I figure I get it on a semi-regular basis then maybe I'll be able to concentrate a little better.

JEFF. Sure you will. I get a little crazy myself if I'm not getting it—

ALAN. And what the hell are you gonna do? Self-stimulation is a one-way street—

BEN. I agree. I can't get into masturbation unless there's a genuine emotional commitment. It can't be just a physical thing with me—

JEFF. Ben? Shut up. *(beat)* So get yourself a woman, Alan.

ROXANNE. *(on intercom)* Alan? There's a Mr. Chevette at Central Reception for you. Shall I have him sent over?

JEFF. That's him, the media guy.

ALAN. *(to the intercom)* Tell them to send him over. *(to BEN and JEFF:)* Holiday Inn, huh? *(ALAN Exits.)*

JEFF. It's getting tough to walk around here with all the bodies.

BEN. How much more time do you give Alan?

JEFF. What time have you got?

BEN. You really think he's through?

JEFF. The fucking guy has started to see Nixon. That's not going to help him professionally.

BEN. He's grieving, Jeff.

JEFF. Alan is a corpse, you could hear it in Dave's voice. He'll slice off Alan's nuts and put'em on his cereal. Alan's going to be sixty-five years old and singing in the Vienna Boys Choir.

(CROSS FADE to ALAN'S office. ALAN is at his desk. ROXANNE Enters with GARY CHEVETTE, the media consultant, late thirties, wearing leather.)

ROXANNE. Alan? This is Gary Chevette—

GARY. —the film-maker. How ya doin'?

ALAN. Hello, Gary. Make yourself comfortable. *(GARY makes himself overly comfortable.)* Would you like something? Coffee?

GARY. How 'bout a sandwich.

ROXANNE. A sandwich?

GARY. Yeah, I missed breakfast. Let's do roast beef on rye, lettuce, tomato, easy on the mayo, a big Coke with ice, do I want fries or chips? Either fries or chips, whatever, don't go to any trouble. Thanks, doll.

ROXANNE. No problem. *(leaves)*

ALAN. So, you and Jeff went to college—

GARY. Oh, yeah, about four hundred years ago. Jeff was a wild-man back then. My absolute five-star memory of Jeffrey is one morning, like six A.M., he's bare-ass, puking his guts out his dorm window, get this, on the sixth floor. We used to call him "Ralph" 'cause he was always losing it like that, you know, RALPH... *(Makes vomit sound.)* as in vomit, so did you get a chance to look at my reel?

ALAN. It hasn't arrived yet—

GARY. Fuckin' U.P.S. Honest to God. I sent it last Monday, right after Jeff called.

ALAN. Well, maybe you could tell me a little bit about what you do.

GARY. I'm a film-maker. I make movies.

ALAN. And Jeff seemed to think you might be able to help us—

GARY. Let me put it this way. I've done the art thing. Now I'm into making money. And believe me, it's working, it's working, thank you, thank you. Commercials, industrials, music videos, you name it. I even coach executives on public speaking. Give me an hour's time and I'll make you look good at a meeting.

ALAN. Sounds like a good business.

GARY. Alan, it's a great business.

ALAN. What we need here is a very specific approach. On January tenth we've got to mobilize our entire national sales staff to push our new anti-hypertensive product. Jeff's feeling was that we've lagged behind the competition in our use of video technology—

GARY. I'm going to say one word, Alan, and that word is the key to what you're talking about. Teleconference.

ALAN. Teleconference?

GARY. Listen to me, Alan. We line up hotels in major cities all over the country, we set up video monitors, get the sales staff in there. They get the rah-rah from the regional sales managers, then bang, the screen comes alive with all these executives. Here's Joe Shmoe, president of the company, talking about the importance of the drug to the nation, here's bippity-bop with the incentive plan, and here's Alan Baylor live from New Jersey with a warm personal appeal...then, bang! We're into a movie, and Alan, it's a fucking great movie, *cinema verité*, handheld cameras, overlapping sound, the whole bit, maybe we go all-out and do it in black and white. And do you know what this movie is? Bringing Maxolan-3000 to the American people. I film in here, the tension, the anguish, the exhilaration, bang bang bang, and we take these salespeople on a roller coaster ride that will leave them with one thought—it's up to them to sell the drug and give the movie a happy ending. Because everybody loves a happy ending, for Chrissakes, I bet Charles Manson loves a happy ending. It's like...people at work for a noble cause. Like World War Two. And do you know something, Alan? Do you mind if I call you Alan? It's a tribute to you. Because I look at you and I see a proud man who has led with dignity for many, many years. And I think we can be honest, how many more years can a man of your age expect to work? Speaking frankly. What I'm saying is, Alan, this is your legacy. A tangible record of what you have done with your life, so people will remember you when you're gone. Christ, I am getting very excited about this project. Any time I can inject a little truth, hell, I sleep better at night. but that's just me, that's who I am, and I don't mind admitting I have a conscience, unlike most of the snakes in the business world—

(ROXANNE Enters with the sandwich and drink.)

GARY. This is a large coke?
ROXANNE. They only have one size—
GARY. Look at this, Alan. Large coke. And we wonder why the Japs are kicking our ass. *(To ROXANNE.)* My fault, I should have ordered two. Thanks, doll.
ALAN. You've certainly given me a lot to think about, Gary. I'll get back to you as soon as possible.
ROXANNE. We have a lounge where you can finish that, Mr. Chevette—
GARY. Oh, no. I'll stay right here with Alan. We're getting along great, right, Alan?

(CROSS FADE to conference room. DIANE and ROXANNE are finishing the party decorations. They are stringing a sign that says "Farewell Carl.")

ACT I   **THE DOWNSIDE**

ROXANNE. So are you going to wait for Bob if he goes to Tibet?

DIANE. I don't know. I've already invested so much time into this relationship. God, I make it sound like a money market.

ROXANNE. Do you go out with other guys when he isn't around?

DIANE. Of course! *(beat)* Well, not all that much. Actually never. *(beat)* Sometimes I wish I could be you for one night.

ROXANNE. Me? You want to be more like me?

DIANE. You always seem to be having fun and not worrying about it too much.

ROXANNE. Well I wish I was more like you. In a job that's going someplace—

DIANE. Believe me, I've made far too many sacrifices for this job.

ROXANNE. So if you want to be me for one night, why don't you come over tonight? We'll go out to this great little bar I know where it's super-easy to meet people—

DIANE. Tonight?

ROXANNE. Why not? Mark and Todd are going winter camping this week-end. I'm not going to just sit home. Did you have other plans?

DIANE. I really should—

ROXANNE. Besides work?

DIANE. What kind of bar is it? I mean, what should I wear?

ROXANNE. Don't worry, I've got some clothes that'll do you fine for one night.

(CROSS FADE to BEN'S office. The PHONE rings.)

BEN. *(on phone)* Hi, Alan. What? Ten minutes? I'll be there. Oh, Alan? Thanks, I really appreciate it. *(hangs up)* Fantastic!

(CROSS FADE to JEFF'S office. JEFF is at his desk. GARY CHEVETTE Enters with video equipment.)

JEFF. So it went well?
GARY. You know me, Jeff. I could sell love beads to a terrorist.
JEFF. So there's a deal.
GARY. Nothing is signed, but assuming I can clear up my schedule we'll put the deal to bed. Today I'll just scout locations.
JEFF. Excellent.

(BEN Enters.)

JEFF. Hey, Ben.
BEN. You got a minute, Jeff?
JEFF. Sure. This is Gary...Ben...
BEN. Oh, the media guy.
GARY. Film-maker. I'll be here right through the launch—
BEN. Anything in particular you're after?
GARY. Just normal stuff—
BEN. That could be a problem around here—
JEFF. So what is it, Ben?
BEN. *(nodding to the door)* Jeff?

JEFF. It's okay, Ben, he's got a job to do. *(Gary picks up the video camera and starts shooting.)*

BEN. *(to JEFF:)* I heard from the old man.

JEFF. Yeah?

BEN. Looks like it's me.

JEFF. For the big office? *(They are both aware that GARY is shooting.)* That's great, Ben. That is really great. I'm really happy for you.

BEN. It could have been you, Jeff. You know that—

JEFF. What the hell. As long as it's one of us.

BEN. I gotta go see him.

JEFF. Congratulations, Ben. You deserve it. *(BEN Exits. GARY is still shooting.)* That's enough, Gary. I've got work to do. You'll have to leave. *(GARY Exits. JEFF throws a wild temper tantrum.)*

JEFF. Fucking son of a bitch! Lucky bastard!

(CROSS FADE to ALAN'S office. BEN and ALAN are meeting.)

ALAN. How far do we go back, Ben?

BEN. Eight years?

ALAN. A long time. I haven't worked with many people who had your ability.

BEN. Thank you, Alan. I've gotta say, working with you has been a really extraordinary experience. I've learned a lot.

ALAN. The combination of your talent and personality really sets you apart from the group.

BEN. I appreciate that, Alan. I hope there's some truth in it.

ALAN. Oh, there's a lot of truth in it. But there's more to our business than talent and personality. One of our greatest commodities is enthusiasm. That's what we must communicate, and if we don't have it ourselves, then how are we going to communicate it?

BEN. That's a good point, Alan.

ALAN. Then there's the question of image. What kind of image do we project? Because we are not poets, struggling for truth in our lonely garret. We are in the image business. When our image suffers, it makes our job that much tougher.

BEN. I'm in total agreement with your management philosophy, Alan. I feel that I could carry on the tradition you've established while bringing my own vision—

ALAN. When we go to Palm Springs for the sales convention we have to be at our best. When we are out there playing golf with corporate, that is every bit as important as what we do here in this office. And when we bring our wives, they are part of the team. Their behavior reflects on us.

BEN. Alan, these business things make my wife very nervous. When she gets nervous she tends to drink too much.

ALAN. That's expected, for Chrissakes, it's practically required. Everyone drinks too much. You want to drink, great. You want to pass out, terrific. You want to go out and crack up your car and wake up in a ditch, fabulous.

BEN. So what's your point?

ALAN. Your wife. Your wife is my point.

BEN. What about my wife, Alan?

ALAN. She's a little too high spirited. Dave called me on this. Flirting with corporate is one thing, that's a feather in your cap, that's a wife who helps her husband's career.

BEN. She doesn't like being thirty-five years old. She'd rather be twenty-two so she acts like she is, especially if she's been drinking—

ALAN. She went over the line, Ben. More than once. Guys talk about this stuff. They brag. Sometimes they don't tell the truth. But we look at the facts, we see you passed out in the bar, we hear about a couple of guys in a room, more than a couple to be absolutely honest, now hell, I'm no prude and neither is Dave, but this is an image problem—

BEN. I'm not even with her anymore, Alan.

ALAN. That's worse. A bad marriage is something to hold onto. No marriage, I don't know...

BEN. You called me in here to talk about my wife?

ALAN. I called you in because I want to give you the opportunity to start over at another company.

BEN. Alan. What are you saying to me?

ALAN. It's a numbers game, you know that. I could have saved you, even with your bad attitude, if Dave didn't get on your case. You get on his bad side and how are you going to move in the corporation? I'm saving you treading water for five years. *(beat)* I'm sorry, Ben. This would be a helluva lot easier if I didn't like you so much.

BEN. I can't believe you're doing this to me, Alan.

(CROSS FADE to JEFF'S office, which is messed up from his tan-

trum. STAN Enters.)

STAN. Jeff? I outlined my ideas for the launch the way you wanted. Do you have time to take a look?

JEFF. *(glancing at the paper)* This is how you've spent your time here.

STAN. I'd certainly welcome your advice in fleshing this out a bit—

JEFF. This is the Stan Oates launch plan.

STAN. In a really abbreviated form.

JEFF. Do you know what you're doing? You're wasting my time, you're wrecking my career, and you're taking food out of my baby daughter's mouth—

STAN. If you don't like the general concepts—

JEFF. You know what I think of the general concepts? *(JEFF rears back and punches STAN in the jaw. STAN drops to the floor.)* Get out of my office.

(CROSS FADE to the conference room, decorated for the party. There's a punch bowl, an artificial Christmas tree, and Christmas carols from a tape player. A single present is on the table. GARY CHEVETTE is checking it out. DIANE and ROXANNE Enter.)

GARY. Hey. How's it going?

ROXANNE. Mr. Chevette? This is Diane Fisk.

GARY. Hi, Diane.

DIANE. Jeff says you've won some awards for your films?

GARY. Sure, the awards are nice. But what matters to me is my own growth and development, both as an artist and as a human being. *(Nodding to the punchbowl.)* So...can I buy anybody a drink?

DIANE. No thanks.

ROXANNE. You think everyone forgot about the party?

DIANE. Who knows? This whole work routine is getting out of control. They'll probably end up postponing the launch anyway.

(ALAN Enters.)

GARY. Hey, Big Guy.

ROXANNE. Merry Christmas, Alan.

ALAN. You're a smart lady, Diane. What would you do if a former President of the United States started calling you up all the time? At first, I'm excited, like anyone would be, I mean I have a lot of questions I want to ask Nixon. But the man will not shut up. He may be a lot of things, and he's definitely an intelligent man, but he is a goddawful listener. The phone rings in the middle of the night I know I'll be up talking to Nixon for a good hour or so. Never get a word in edgewise. Nixon this, Nixon that.

DIANE. Do you want some punch, Alan?

(She gets ALAN some punch. JEFF Enters.)

JEFF. I'm afraid I've got some bad news. Stan won't be at the party.

ROXANNE. Why not?

JEFF. I heard a crash outside the men's room. It seems

he took a really bad fall, you know how he is, a little clumsy. So I got him right down to the infirmary.

ROXANNE. Should we go see if he's alright?

JEFF. Can't see him for a while. Don't worry, he's in good hands. Has everybody met Gary Chevette? We're counting on Gary for a terrific Maxolan teleconference. *(JEFF gets some punch.)* Great party, Roxanne.

(CARL Enters.)

CARL. Ho ho ho! Hi everybody! *(Silence. Then DIANE shakes his hand.)*

DIANE. I've really enjoyed working with you, Carl.

JEFF. *(Shakes CARL'S hand.)* Carl.

ROXANNE. *(Kisses CARL.)* We'll sure miss you.

CARL. Thanks. Merry Christmas everybody.

ROXANNE. "Merry Christmas." I've always liked that about you, Carl. The stiff upper lip. *(CARL gets some punch.)*

DIANE. Where's Ben?

JEFF. He wasn't in his office.

ROXANNE. I think we better get this thing going. With the snowstorm I don't know how long people will stay. *(handing CARL the present)* Carl?

CARL. For me? Wow, I'm really touched. *(CARL turns and sees the sign "Farewell Carl.")*

DIANE. It's the least we could do.

JEFF. And believe me, we wanted to do the least for you. Only kidding, Carl.

CARL. I bet Stan is behind this.

ROXANNE. Why Stan?

CARL. He's the only one I told about my ski-trip to Utah. I sure didn't expect such a send-off. *(CARL opens the present, a briefcase.)* Thanks a lot. Really. This is, boy, I don't know...I've never had friends like this...

(BEN Enters.)

CARL. Thanks, Ben. I know you're part of this—
BEN. Part of what?
CARL. My going away party.
BEN. Where are you going?
CARL. Skiing in Utah.
BEN. That's nice, Carl. But you can give me the fucking briefcase! *(BEN grabs the briefcase.)*
JEFF. Ben!
CARL. It's mine! They gave it to me!
BEN. Yeah, well I'm the one that got fired! I want the present!
DIANE. You got fired?
ALAN. Ben is through at this company. We wish you all the best, Ben.
JEFF. My God, Ben. I thought you got promoted—
ROXANNE. When did this happen?
BEN. Fuck it. You know what I'm saying? Just fuck it.
ALAN. *(raising his glass)* Fuck it.
JEFF. *(to BEN:)* Man, I feel so bad for you. I was just thinking how great it was about the promotion.
CARL. *(grabbing the briefcase)* It had my name on the card, Ben—
ROXANNE. *(grabbing it back, then tossing it to BEN)* The

present is not for you, Carl, okay?

CARL. *(grabbing it back from BEN)* But I wanted—

DIANE. *(grabbing it from CARL and handing it to BEN)* Shut up, Carl. Ben, I don't know what to say.

(BEN is clutching the briefcase. We hear DAVE'S voice from the speaker.)

DAVE. Happy holidays, everyone.

ALAN. *(turning to the speaker)* Dave! Good to see you!

DAVE. Central switchboard put me through. I just wanted to wish everyone all the best for the holidays. I know how hard you've been working—

BEN. *(giving the speaker the finger)* Merry Christmas, Dave! My wife sends her best, too!

DAVE. Thanks, Jeff. I've just been sitting here on the plane brain-storming—

(We hear COMMOTION in the background on the speaker.)

DAVE. My flight is getting in to Newark in a couple of hours and I'll be coming straight to the office, so Alan, if we could meet—

ALAN. There's a hulluva storm here, Dave. We're all going home a little early—

(In the background on the speaker we hear VOICES screaming in Spanish.)

DAVE. *(utterly calm)* That's okay, there seems to be a bit of a hijacking in progress so I'll have to sign off. I'll call

ACT I   **THE DOWNSIDE**   53

you at home, Alan, and for all the rest of you, enjoy your holidays and keep up the good work. Let's be thankful for all we have during this joyful holiday season—

(A GUNSHOT and a SCREAM, then the speaker goes dead.)

ALAN. Dave? Dave, are you okay?

(The OTHERS crowd around the speaker and stare at it with concern. BLACKOUT.)

END OF ACT I, SCENE 2

Scene 3

Monday morning after Christmas. LIGHTS up on the reception area. ROXANNE is at a computer terminal. DIANE Enters from outside.

DIANE. You're starting early today.
ROXANNE. Just trying to confirm all the hotels for the teleconference. This is turning into an organizational nightmare. *(DIANE gets a cup of coffee.)*
DIANE. Christmas okay?
ROXANNE. Pretty painless this year. Did Bob make up his mind?
DIANE. Tibet, but he wants me to wait for him.
ROXANNE. And?

DIANE. Who knows? Whatever happened with that guy you were with?

ROXANNE. At the bar? Oh, he was such a sweetheart. We went to his cabin out in the woods. He had a jeep which is the only way we made it through the snow. Once we got there he built a fire and we cuddled in front of it, he undressed me so slowly...then he took off his clothes and we lay on this sheepskin rug with the storm roaring outside. It was glorious.

DIANE. Are you going to see him again?

ROXANNE. Oh, God no. He's happily married. *(beat)* What about you? I've been dying to ask about the guy you left with that night—

DIANE. Oh, he was nice. I'm so glad you got me out of my apartment—

ROXANNE. What did you do?

DIANE. Nothing much.

ROXANNE. Did you spend the night with him?

DIANE. That's really my business, Roxie.

ROXANNE. Diane, I tell you everything.

DIANE. I had a good time, okay? *(ROXANNE turns back to her work.)* I keep thinking about Ben. Out of everyone we lost this year—

ROXANNE. He's in his office.

DIANE. Really? Why is he still there?

(CROSS FADE to outside BEN'S office. DIANE knocks on the door.)

DIANE. Ben?
BEN. Yeah?

DIANE. It's me.

(No response. She Enters and turns on the LIGHTS. BEN is just waking up. The office is a shambles.)

DIANE. Jesus, Ben. Look at this place. *(Hands him her coffee.)* You need this more than I do.

BEN. It must be Monday.

DIANE. You didn't spend Christmas here, did you?

BEN. Yeah, I drank eggnog, sang carols, gave myself a present...

DIANE. You were alone?

BEN. I split with my wife, Diane.

DIANE. I know, but I thought you'd be with family.

BEN. What can I say, this is it. Death runs in my family, Diane.

DIANE. I wish I'd known you were alone. Over the holidays I've had all this shit going on with Bob and my parents and everything else, and Christmas night I just burst into tears, I mean I never do that. My sister asked me what was wrong and you know what I said? I said "they fired Ben." I didn't even know I was going to say it, it just popped out.

BEN. I'm glad I could take part in your holiday joy.

DIANE. How long are you going to stay here?

BEN. As long as it takes. Alan is on his way out. Jeff will get the big office and put me back on the pay-roll.

DIANE. Why do you think Jeff will get the job?

BEN. Who else is there?

DIANE. Thanks. Ben.

BEN. Hey, I'm sorry, Diane. I just thought—

DIANE. A man will get it. Naturally.

BEN. Don't start, Diane. I feel bad enough already.

DIANE. If it's any consolation, I know someone who had a worse Christmas than you.

BEN. Who's that?

DIANE. Dave. They hijacked his plane.

BEN. I know.

DIANE. And they blew it up. Now Dave is a hostage.

BEN. Bummer. Is Alan here?

DIANE. Not yet.

BEN. Great. Maybe I can get something to eat.

DIANE. Ben? As long as you're living here, do you want to get out for a while later on? We could go to Chico's or someplace, my treat—

BEN. Thanks, Diane, but there are people I'd rather not run into at Chico's.

DIANE. Oh, well, what are you going to do tonight?

BEN. I don't know. Prob'ly go out and try to find a woman. *(BEN leaves his office, still in his bathrobe. DIANE stares after him, hurt.)*

(CROSS FADE to reception area. ROXANNE is still working at the terminal. JEFF Enters from outside at the same time that BEN Enters from the hall. BEN gets a donut from the counter and starts back to his office.)

JEFF. Ben! *(BEN stops, sees JEFF, then continues toward his office. JEFF follows.)* Look at yourself, Ben—

BEN. I'd rather not.

JEFF. You can't walk around here like that. *(They are in BEN'S office.)*

BEN. Leave me alone, Jeff. I just want everybody to leave me alone, okay?

JEFF. Let me help you out. Go to my house, get cleaned up—

BEN. You've helped enough already.

JEFF. What's that s'posed to mean?

BEN. I went to that Holiday Inn you were talking about. I even struck out there.

JEFF. They're hookers, Ben. They've got no reason to play hard to get.

BEN. You know how that makes me feel? Chat up a prostitute and get a drink thrown in my face?

JEFF. Wait a second, where was this place?

BEN. The Holiday Inn near the airport, like you said, on 17.

JEFF. On 17?

BEN. Right.

JEFF. That's the wrong one, Ben. I was talking about the one on Airport Road. The Holiday Inn you went to, I go by it every morning on the way to work. They always have conventions there. Right now it's parole officers, it's right on the sign.

BEN. Great. Parole officers.

JEFF. Jesus, I wonder how Alan did?

(CROSS FADE to the reception area, where ROXANNE is working. JEFF Enters.)

ROXANNE. Jeff? I thought it would be a good idea if we sent Stan some flowers. He was in the hospital for three days and they had to wire his jaw. So if everyone kicks in ten dollars—

JEFF. You know, these office collections are really getting out of hand. We give Carl a going away present when he isn't going anywhere, now you want me to send flowers to this jerk who probably won't last six months—

(STAN Enters. His jaw is wired shut and a neck brace prevents him from talking. JEFF doesn't see him.)

JEFF. I say, ten dollars is ten dollars and we've got to draw the line with Stan—
ROXANNE. Morning, Stan!
JEFF. *(Turns and sees him.)* Stanley! How are you, buddy?
ROXANNE. Are you okay? We're all so sorry about your accident. We didn't think you'd be in today.
JEFF. Here, let me get you some coffee.

(JEFF gets STAN some coffee. ALAN Enters.)

ALAN. Morning everybody. Stanley! How are we feeling today?
STAN. *(unintelligible response)*
ALAN. Good to hear, good to hear. Jeff has told me what he saw, maybe the floors did have too much wax, but we've got an excellent health plan as you well know. Anything you do in the nature of legal action is obviously up to you. I'm going to put you in Ben's old office, a step up, a sign of good faith, a better place to work—
JEFF. Ben is still in his office.
ALAN. What do you mean? How long does it take him

ACT I   **THE DOWNSIDE**   59

to clean out his desk?

ROXANNE. He doesn't seem to be leaving.

ALAN. He has to leave! He's fired! My office, Jeff.

(CROSS FADE to the conference room. GARY is videotaping CARL'S interview.)

CARL. What do I like about my job? The challenge. Every morning facing the unknown. It's like being in the wilderness. My wife believes in reincarnation. She thinks I was some kind of savage warrior in a previous lifetime, and I guess I'd have to agree with that. I see myself in animal skins, loping across a field at daybreak with spear in hand. That kind of background has really helped me here at Mark & Maxwell.

GARY. You believe in reincarnation?

CARL. I said my wife does.

GARY. What about you?

CARL. The point is, if I did believe in reincarnation, yes, I would definitely believe I once was a savage warrior.

GARY. Do you believe in God? *(GARY moves in close, putting the camera in CARL'S face.)*

CARL. Is this film going to be seen by the entire sales staff?

(CROSS FADE to ALAN's office. ALAN and JEFF are meeting.)

ALAN. This is the problem with Ben. He won't play by the rules. The rules are, you get fired you leave your office.

JEFF. I don't know why you let him go, Alan.

ALAN. Because I had to get rid of somebody. Dave made me hire Stan and that meant I had to lose somebody.

JEFF. You keep Carl and you fire Ben—

ALAN. Look, if I have to say who is better, Ben Davis or Carl Hastings, the answer is obvious.

(LIGHTS UP on BEN and CARL. Their PHONES RING at the mention of their names because of the voice-activated phone system. They pick up their phones.)

JEFF. Then why did you fire Ben?

ALAN. He's got an attitude problem. He's got a wife who fools around, he's got mobsters after him, Jeff, this is not a half-way house we're running here. I don't think Ben can help us with this launch, and if we blow this one, we're all out of a job.

JEFF. Carl is like a piece of furniture. He sits in there and no work ever comes out. He has no opinions on anything but sports—

ALAN. He plays golf. He can talk for hours at a party and not say a goddamn thing. He looks good in a suit. I don't have to discuss this with you. I just want a solution to get Ben out of his office.

JEFF. How about the National Guard?

ALAN. I like Ben. It hurt me to do this, Jeff.

JEFF. The fact is he's going through a rough time. He's living in his office. Plus, he feels safe from his bookie.

ALAN. Wonderful. So now I'm not just taking away his

job but his house, too. Plus endangering his life.

JEFF. Why don't you put him on probation or make him a consultant for a while? Give the guy a break?

ALAN. Jeff? I don't want to be the reason this company fails.

JEFF. How is that possible?

ALAN. You don't have to worry about that. All you have to worry about is the launch. If you need me I'll be on the eleventh floor all day. They've got their hands full with Dave out. *(ALAN puts a folder in the file cabinet and leaves. As soon as he's gone, JEFF opens the file cabinet and starts reading from the folder.)*

(LIGHTS UP on BEN'S office. He wraps himself in his blanket and stealthily makes his way down the hall to ALAN'S office, where JEFF is reading the report.)

BEN. You trying out the big office? Seeing how it fits?

JEFF. *(He looks up, startled.)* Ben! What are you doing here?

BEN. Just wanted to thank you for sticking up for me with the old man.

JEFF. How'd you know?

BEN. The intercom kicked in. I heard the whole meeting.

JEFF. Jesus—

BEN. Don't worry, you didn't trash me.

JEFF. I was trying to think—

BEN. I know you were. *(beat)* So what are you doing here, waiting for Nixon to call?

JEFF. Research. I'm supposed to be reaching out to the so-called innovators in the field, and I need ammunition.

BEN. Bullshit. *(BEN takes the folder.)* You finding anything good? *(BEN is scanning a report. JEFF wants to stop him, but it's too late.)*

JEFF. Not really. *(beat)* Actually there's some pretty heavy shit in here.

BEN. *(reading the paper)* Jesus Christ...does anyone know about this?

JEFF. That's the old man's department. He must have had a reason for not telling us. Maybe this Dr. Ryan is bonkers. Maybe this is just not a problem. If Maxolan-3000 is the same drug they've been using in Europe—

BEN. The same except for that slight reformulation we're doing for manufacturing reasons. And this doctor seems to think it's more than slight...and that there are some real health questions involved...disorientation ...Jesus.

JEFF. That's one doctor. All the others give it the green light.

BEN. The old man must have figured this gets out, the launch gets delayed. So he sits on it.

JEFF. There's going to be a difference of opinion with any new product. I bet there are letters like this for every drug on the market. If we don't go for it, some other company will, and they'll clean up. What's the alternative? More R & D? Third-world it for a while? Either way we lose the U.S. market.

BEN. Jesus. So what are you going to do?

JEFF. The people upstairs decide what the risks are. I'll

take it up with them. Or maybe I'll try to get in touch with Dave directly.

BEN. You mean you're going over Alan's head?

JEFF. What choice do I have? We've got everything riding on this, Ben. Besides, it's a chance to help a friend.

BEN. Help a friend?

JEFF. Hey, do you want your job back or not?

BEN. I need this job, Jeff. This is the best place I ever lived.

(JEFF Exits with the report. LIGHTS UP on JEFF in his office with the report, and BEN, still in ALAN'S office, in his blanket. BLACKOUT.)

END OF ACT I

ACT II

Scene 1

The next morning. LIGHTS UP on the reception area. ROXANNE is collating piles of paper. BEN enters, wearing his bathrobe. He has more paper for Roxanne.

ROXANNE. Thanks, Ben.
BEN. No problem. The rest should be done in about ten minutes. *(beat)* There's something I've been meaning to ask you.
ROXANNE. Sure, anything.
BEN. What line works best on you?
ROXANNE. What line works best on me?
BEN. You're in a bar, some guy comes over and says, "Can I buy you a drink?" or "I like your smile" or "Hey, babe, let's get married." What line works?
ROXANNE. Depends on the guy, the situation, what kind of mood I'm in, mainly something honest, like, "I'd really like to talk to you."
BEN. Honesty. Jeez, I never even thought of that.

(DIANE Enters from outside.)

DIANE. Morning, everybody. Morning, Roxanne. *(ROXANNE ignores her.)*

ACT II   **THE DOWNSIDE**   65

BEN. Diane, what line works if you want to get picked up?

DIANE. Why? Are you having problems?

BEN. Me? No, I'm just wondering.

DIANE. What line have you been trying, Ben?

BEN. I have a couple of drinks and then I go up to some girl and say, "Please save me."

DIANE. Please save me? What do they do?

BEN. They look away. Then they sneak a glance back, the way you look at a terrible car accident without really wanting to. What would you do if some guy tried that line, Diane?

DIANE. Wish I'd stayed home. *(DIANE Exits to her office.)*

BEN. What's wrong with her?

ROXANNE. I think everyone's feeling the squeeze.

(BEN starts for his office just as ALAN Enters.)

ALAN. Ben! *(BEN stops.)* You've been avoiding me, Ben. I fired you last week and you're still here.

BEN. I've been helping Roxanne.

ALAN. What do you want me to do? Call security?

BEN. Leave me alone.

ALAN. You plan to just stay here?

BEN. Just 'til I get an apartment.

ALAN. You can't stay. Corporate made the numbers clear.

BEN. Do what you have to do, Alan. Call security.

ALAN. You know I don't want to do that.

BEN. Then let me consult for a while. 'Til I get a place.

ALAN. Goddammit, Ben. Just get dressed. That's all I ask. *(BEN Exits to his office. ALAN watches ROXANNE working.)* I can't even go bowling any more. Last night I was out with a couple of buddies, I get up there to bowl, two alleys to the right that son of a bitch is bowling up a storm. By himself. You gotta be damn serious to go bowling by yourself.

ROXANNE. Who's that, Alan?

ALAN. Nixon. I'll give him this, he's a helluva good bowler.

(JEFF Enters.)

JEFF. Morning everybody. Alan, have you got time to meet today?

ALAN. Any word from Dave, Roxie?

ROXANNE. Apparently all the passengers are being held hostage—

ALAN. Good God! Dave is a hostage? Will he be at the meeting?

ROXANNE. He said he'd try. The Coast Guard is supposed to pick them up this morning. Unless there's a battle he'll call—

ALAN. Fine. Jeff, you and I had better meet right now. *(JEFF and ALAN go to ALAN'S office.)* I've got a guy wandering around in his bathrobe. I've got a guy who can't talk, and I've got a week to do a job we thought we had six months to do. It's a fucking zoo.

JEFF. I'm thinking the same thing.

ALAN. What do we do?

JEFF. We look at the reasons for this lack of control.

ALAN. You mean the time pressure.

JEFF. I mean the leadership vacuum.

ALAN. Leadership vacuum?

JEFF. The guy at the top sets the tone for the whole plant.

ALAN. Are you saying I'm not doing my job?

JEFF. I think the whole thrust of this kind of work is changing. We need to streamline our relationship with sales. We need to reach them more directly. We need to—

ALAN. Hey. Jeffrey, I brought you in here. I taught you this business from the ground up. I did that because I saw a great deal of potential. But I will not let you tell me how to do my job.

JEFF. The best thing you could do for the company is step down, Alan. It hurts me to say this.

ALAN. Why are you telling me this, Jeff?

JEFF. I think you should retire before you take the rest of us down with you.

ALAN. You can't talk that way to me.

JEFF. Are you going to fire me?

ALAN. I'd do it. I fired Ben.

JEFF. Didn't make much difference.

ALAN. I say the word and your career is over. I swear to God I'm ready to do that.

JEFF. I bet you would, Alan. You get to be a certain age, your mind starts to go—

ALAN. Get the fuck out of here.

JEFF. You had a choice, Alan. You could have dealt with Ryan's tests on Maxolan. Gone to FDA, done the right thing. But you decided to sit on them. Get the approval, hope the drug is a big seller, go out in a blaze of glory.

ALAN. How do you know about this?

JEFF. *(putting the report on the desk)* Your failure to act is at least negligent, at worst criminal.

ALAN. For Chrissakes, it was all delayed! By the time I got this we'd put so much money into the launch there was no way I could turn back. I did it for the company—

JEFF. You'll have to tell that to corporate. What's Dave gonna think, hiding a report indicating a possible downside to our biggest product launch ever? You're through, Alan. You fight me on this and it will all come out. I'm giving you the opportunity to go quietly, with dignity, and save this company you served for forty years.

ALAN. You fuck. You come to my house. I got a pair of pistols. We'll go out back in my woods and we'll finish this thing like men.

JEFF. You put a lot of people at risk, Alan. That's not right.

ALAN. I swear to God I wouldn't ask anyone else to take a risk I wouldn't take myself.

JEFF. I'll see you at the meeting, Alan. *(JEFF Exits.)*

(CROSS FADE to the conference room. ROXANNE is setting up for the meeting. DIANE Enters.)

DIANE. Okay, I'll tell you. I brought him to my apartment. We slept together and it was okay, mainly because it meant somebody was really paying attention to me for a change. In the morning he didn't look so great and he wasn't so charming and I couldn't wait for him to leave. That's what happened, Roxie, and you were right, I should have told you since you tell me everything.

ROXANNE. And you feel lousy about it, right?

DIANE. Just sort of stupid, like what's the point? I mean I'm lying there in bed on Saturday morning with this guy I don't know and we're having this incredibly stilted conversation about our jobs and it all seemed just a little ridiculous, you know?

ROXANNE. What are you after, Diane? Are you going to wait a whole year for Bob to stop meditating?

DIANE. I guess I am if the alternative is one-night stands. God, there are so many jerks out there. I'd rather be alone.

ROXANNE. There's absolutely no guy you really like right now?

DIANE. Well...

ROXANNE. Who?

DIANE. There is, but there's a problem.

ROXANNE. Who is it?

DIANE. Ben.

ROXANNE. Ben? What's the problem?

DIANE. Ben. Ben is also the problem. Here's this guy that I really like, God know why, and he acts like...last night I offered to take him out to dinner and he said he was going to go find a woman instead. Do you know how that makes me feel?

ROXANNE. You better zap him, Diane. Give him a jolt.

DIANE. How do I give him a jolt?

ROXANNE. Ignore him, insult him, whatever it takes.
DIANE. What's that going to do?
ROXANNE. Make him notice you. He'll stop taking you for granted.
DIANE. I can't do that. His life is such a mess. His wife booted him out, he got fired—
ROXANNE. Believe me, if you ever want to be more than just friends, you'll kick him in the face and leave him crawling in the gutter.

(CARL and STAN Enter. ROXANNE goes to the telephone to try to make the connection with DAVE.)

DIANE. Did you have a chance to review the learning systems, Carl?
CARL. Not yet. I want to give them my fullest attention—
DIANE. I need them tomorrow.
CARL. No sweat.

(JEFF Enters.)

JEFF. Have you got him, Roxie?
ROXANNE. I'm trying.

(ALAN Enters and takes a seat at the table.)

CARL. I had a question, Alan—
ALAN. Can't you see I'm busy, Carl?

(ALAN is sitting perfectly still. BEN Enters in his bathrobe.)

ALAN. Couldn't you at least get dressed for the meeting, Ben?
BEN. All my clothes are at the laundry.
ROXANNE. I've got him! Everybody ready?
JEFF. Go ahead, Roxie.

(DAVE'S voice is heard on the speaker, as calm and efficient as ever.)

DAVE. Morning everybody.

(MUMBLED "good mornings." In the background on the speaker we hear CHANTING CROWDS, SCREAMS, CONFUSION.)

ALAN. Dave, are you alright?
DAVE. Terrific, Alan, thanks. I may have to break this off at any point. It seems we're in a bit of a hostage situation at the present time. From what I hear, we're getting some random torture activity, nothing major. To continue my comments from last time, the board is in agreement at our positioning of Maxolan in the market. My point to you concerns security. It's imperative that we maintain absolute secrecy on this until we're ready for the blitzkrieg. I guarantee Lovelle will move up their launch date if they find out what we're up to. FDA approval is in my pocket.
JEFF. Any chance you'll be here for the launch, Dave?
DAVE. Absolutely.

(We hear GUNSHOTS.)

DAVE. There seems to be something of a firefight developing, which means an initial rescue attempt. I have every confidence I'll be with you—

(More SCREAMS and GUNSHOTS from the speaker.)

DAVE. I'd better sign off. Good luck — *(The speaker goes dead.)*

JEFF. Dave? Dave?

BEN. Have a nice day, Dave.

JEFF. Roxie? Keep trying to establish contact, okay?

DIANE. Alan? *Now* is there a chance the launch will be pushed back? I'm asking because of the amount of work we have to do and whether this is a realistic date we're talking about, given... *(She gestures to the speaker.)*

JEFF. Yes, it can be done, and no, we will not move the date back.

DIANE. I was asking Alan.

JEFF. Alan has an announcement to make.

ALAN. I have to tell them now?

JEFF. Go ahead, Alan.

ALAN. *(standing up)* I've decided after much reflection that I must relinquish my responsibilities as Head of Marketing & Sales. I do this reluctantly, because as you all know, I've put in a good many years here and I had looked forward to several more. Unfortunately, health problems make it necessary for me to retire, effective immediately. I have asked Jeff to step in on an interim basis to get us through this difficult period. He has agreed.

DIANE. Alan...are you going to be okay? I mean is it

ACT II   **THE DOWNSIDE**   73

anything serious?

JEFF. I think we can hold the personal questions until a more appropriate time. Right now we have a great deal to accomplish. However, I'd like to take a moment to salute Alan and his many years of meritorious service. Thank you, Alan. From all of us.

ALAN. This has been my home, especially the last few months. You people have been my family. I'm going to miss all this more than any of you know. *(beat)* Jeff, I still have a lot to contribute, and I'm ready to help out any way I can—

JEFF. I'm sorry, Alan, but I must respect Dave's wishes. For security reasons you'd better leave. We can only have employees at a meeting like this.

ALAN. I don't even need a paycheck. I feel I can still contribute—

JEFF. I'll expect you out of the building by noon, Alan.

DIANE. What are you doing, Jeff?

JEFF. My job. I expect each of you to do the same. *(ALAN slowly leaves.)*

DIANE. I don't like the way that was handled.

JEFF. That's how things are going to be. We have a major opportunity here, and I'm not going to let it slip away. Diane, the learning systems on my desk tomorrow morning.

DIANE. Carl still is proof-reading—

JEFF. No excuses. Stan, the confirmations on the hotels are completed?

STAN. *(unintelligible response)*

JEFF. Get on it. Ben, you're still on the speeches?

BEN. Anything you say, boss.

JEFF. Cut out the bull-shit. Put on a suit and talk to corporate so they know what they're going to say. Carl, have you worked out the incentive plan?

CARL. Yes and no.

JEFF. For Chrissakes, Carl, I want an answer.

CARL. We need to talk about some things.

JEFF. So talk.

CARL. I mean, we should have a meeting.

JEFF. We're at a meeting, Carl! Don't sit at a meeting and tell me we should have a meeting. Get on the phone, get what you need and set up the plan. That's what sales wants to hear, you know that.

CARL. Okay.

JEFF. This is for everybody. We're going to have progress reports every morning. I want to know where you're at and how you're spending your time. Ben, stick around a minute, the rest of you, make every minute count. We haven't got much time. *(Everyone leaves the room except BEN and JEFF.)*

BEN. Jesus, man, if you coached the Giants they wouldn't dare lose.

JEFF. Help get us through this, you're back on staff. I'm in a position to do that for you.

BEN. What happened with the old man?

JEFF. Health problems. I guess he saw his doctor. Got a real scare.

BEN. Were you the doctor, Jeff? You give him a scare?

JEFF. There was no deal, Ben. He told me this morning.

BEN. I guess that Maxolan report becomes your responsibility now.

JEFF. Ben? I'm giving you a chance to get your life back together. Don't blow it.

(CROSS FADE to the reception area. ROXANNE is stapling the piles of paper. BEN Enters, still wearing his bathrobe.)

ROXANNE. One of these goes to everyone on the floor. I'll take this over to Stan myself.

BEN. Roxanne? I'd really like to talk to you.

ROXANNE. I'm listening.

BEN. You said you fell for that line. "I'd really like to talk to you." Now you have to go out with me.

ROXANNE. You're not trying to pick me up, are you, Ben?

BEN. Well...yeah, kind of.

ROXANNE. Forget lines, Ben. Be yourself.

BEN. That's the one thing I know doesn't work. Last night I started to get a little crazy here. And I got to thinking that maybe there was still some kind of hope left for my marriage. So I drove over to my house to see if maybe we could, you know, just talk. And there was a strange car in the driveway. Roxie, I want to feel like a human being again.

ROXANNE. I think you oughta spend time with someone you like instead of trying to pick up girls.

BEN. I'm trying to find someone I like. And judging by what's out there it's going to take a long time and a lot of people—

ROXANNE. Maybe you aren't a swinger, Ben. To tell you the truth, I've always seen you as the guy in the kitchen talking sports while everyone else is in the other room ripping off their clothes—

BEN. Now wait a second, I've been around! I've done some things I'm not proud of!

ROXANNE. The point is, maybe you don't have to wander around begging strange women to save you. Maybe there's someone you already know and see every day who is dying to get involved.

BEN. Do you know how good that makes me feel? *(BEN embraces her. She doesn't respond.)*

ROXANNE. Not me, Ben!

BEN. Then who?

ROXANNE. Diane.

BEN. Me and Diane?

ROXANNE. You like her. I can tell.

BEN. Yeah, I like her a lot. But she's like a sister.

ROXANNE. Oh, you and Diane have the same parents—

BEN. No, but—

ROXANNE. Then she's not your sister.

BEN. I just hadn't really thought of her that way. Me and Diane? Is that possible?

ROXANNE. Well maybe if you went out of your way to be nice to her you could find out.

(DIANE Enters.)

BEN. Diane?

DIANE. Can't you see I'm busy?

BEN. I wanted to talk to you.

DIANE. I'm afraid I just don't have time for you and your sad stories, Ben. You're not the only one with problems. *(BEN looks from DIANE to ROXANNE, who quickly Exits. BLACKOUT.)*

(A single LIGHT on ALAN in the conference room. During the following, the LIGHTS come up and we see GARY taping.)

ALAN. There's a moment I remember, thirty years ago, leaving the office. It was the early spring, dusk, and I remember the patches of snow on the ground and the shadows from the trees...the wind rustling the leaves ...everything around me seemed so alive. I was the last one to leave that night and I stood by myself in the parking lot just feeling the night around me and I was filled with this nameless feeling of hope...of faith in all this. I don't even remember what it was, a promotion, my family, I don't know. But I remember that moment better than anything that happened to me in forty years.

GARY. You must feel a lot of pride, all the years you've been here.

ALAN. I gave generously of my time and talents. I helped the company grow. I spent forty years here, but I don't think people will remember me when I'm gone. I never think about the people who left. One day they're gone. Someone else sits in their office. Lately this has accelerated, this turn-over, this rush of faces. I'm just one of them and it's my time to go.

(BLACKOUT)

END OF ACT II, SCENE 1

Scene 2

Monday morning, two weeks later. LIGHTS up on the reception area. ROXANNE, dressed in a conservative business suit, is stapling a memo to the bulletin board. DIANE Enters and looks at the bulletin board.

DIANE. Oh, God, another meeting. You know I feel so bad about the way I've been treating Ben. Maybe it was good advice, but the whole week-end I kept thinking—

(The phone is ringing. ROXANNE makes no move to answer it.)

DIANE. Roxanne? Are you going to get that?
ROXANNE. Central switchboard will get it.
DIANE. Oh. Okay. So did you see Mark or Todd this week-end?
ROXANNE. I broke up with them.
DIANE. Both of them?
ROXANNE. They didn't take it very well. They kept saying they'd never loved anyone as much as they loved me and they thought they could make it work. It's okay, I don't have time for them anymore.

(JEFF Enters in a hurry.)

JEFF. Any word on Dave?

ACT II THE DOWNSIDE 79

ROXANNE. The Coast Guard ship that rescued him was caught in the hurricane. All contact has been temporarily lost.

JEFF. Damn! And he was s'posed to be here for the launch!

DIANE. We've still got another day.

JEFF. I don't know how he'll make it if he's lost at sea. *(Hands ROXANNE a piece of paper.)* Would you type this for me, Roxie? It has to go out today.

ROXANNE. Type it yourself.

JEFF. What?

ROXANNE. You heard me. Type it yourself.

JEFF. Roxanne! *(moving close to her)* I don't want to have to fire you. I think maybe the two of us should go out for a good long lunch and see what kind of a future you have at this company.

DIANE. Leave her alone, Jeff.

JEFF. She doesn't want to be left alone. I know what she wants. *(to ROXANNE:)* I think about you a lot. I have fantasies about you.

ROXANNE. I have fantasies about you, too, Jeff.

JEFF. Really?

ROXANNE. Yeah. I always see you stuck under the wheels of a speeding car.

JEFF. I'll remember that.

(GARY Enters with a video cassette.)

GARY. You trusted me, Jeffrey. It's hard to put a price tag on that.

JEFF. You finished?

GARY. That implies closure, and I'm always open to change. I stayed up three days with this, and there were times, Jeffrey, there were times...and yes, it's running long, close to four hours—

JEFF. Four hours?

GARY. But that was dictated by my own belief in the material. And I have learned from this experience that there is a fine line, a fine fucking line between true genius and utter horseshit, and at two in the morning with the Beastie Boys on the stereo, I crossed that line into genius territory. *(JEFF pulls GARY aside.)*

JEFF. I can't put a four hour film in front of the sales staff. Can't you do something with it?

GARY. Do something with it? You haven't even seen it.

JEFF. For $335,000 I just want something I can use, that's all.

GARY. I aimed too high, I can see that now. You wanted a toy boat and I gave you a nuclear submarine. Now you are upset—

JEFF. I'm not upset. This is not personal. The film is too long.

GARY. Jeffrey, I can't believe this. When you came to me I thought it was because you wanted to bring art and commerce together, where they belong. I thought it was based on your respect for me as an artist. But now you are standing there in your suit and tie ordering me to paint the Sistine Chapel with a roller.

JEFF. I'm not knocking the film, Gary, I haven't even seen it. But you've got to change it around, okay? By tomorrow. Because I'd hate to see you lose your final check after all the work you put in.

GARY. So it's come down to this. Money. Relax. Now that I know where you're coming from I can re-edit the film and bring it down to an acceptable level. I'll use the exteriors of the plant with a voice-over, punch in the interviews, a few lab shots, a couple of boring graphs, music up, inspirational tag, then let the executives make their speeches. No problem, if that's all you want.

JEFF. Fine.

GARY. Hey, you oughta get some rest, Ralph. This job is really beating you up. *(GARY Exits. JEFF starts for his office.)*

DIANE. Jeff? Meeting this morning.

JEFF. Who called it?

DIANE. I don't know.

JEFF. Goddammit, is someone playing games here? Because we don't have the time. I want to see everybody in the conference room.

(STAN and CARL Enter from outside. STAN'S bandage is off. CARL is limping.)

DIANE. Oh, the neck brace is finally off. Can you talk, Stan?

CARL. He can talk up a storm. Just wait.

DIANE. Are you limping, Carl?

CARL. Just in my legs.

DIANE. There's a meeting this morning, Carl.

CARL. I know.

(CROSS FADE to conference room. BEN is reading the real estate

ads. DIANE Enters. BEN looks up, then back at the paper. They make a point of ignoring each other. CARL Enters, limping.)

CARL. You still don't have time for the basketball team, Ben?

BEN. Sorry.

CARL. With Stan hurt we're down to three guys. Last night it got rough and two of our guys fouled out. It ended up me against five very big guys from the mailroom at Lovelle for the whole fourth quarter. No mercy, Ben. One eighty-six to eleven was the final.

BEN. I'm trying to find a place to live, Carl.

(JEFF Enters.)

JEFF. Whatever this is, it better be quick. Who the hell's missing? Where's Stan?

(ROXANNE and STAN Enter.)

JEFF. From now on all meetings must be cleared through me. Is that understood? Now who called this meeting? *(They look around the table at each other.)* If no one called the meeting we can go back to work.

STAN. I called the meeting.

JEFF. This oughta be good. Make it fast, we haven't got a lot of time.

STAN. I just had a few announcements to make. First, I'm pleased to report that Mark & Maxwell has been taken over by the Stewart Corporation. The deal has been in the works under the utmost secrecy for the past month and was completed late last night. This take-over gives Mark & Maxwell greater financial stability and presents truly outstanding career opportunities for all of you. The immediate restructuring will be as follows. Dave is taking over as CEO and I'll be assuming his current duties. Roxanne is moving with me up to the eleventh floor to serve as my administrative assistant. I've been extremely impressed by her efficiency and knowledge of the business. She will be my liaison with this department during the transition period. And Carl will be taking over her duties here. Other than that, I don't plan to make any major personnel changes until after the launch.

JEFF. Stan? What are you talking about? Is this for real?

STAN. I came here as head man in the take-over.

JEFF. You mean...you are the new Dave?

STAN. Right, Jeff. And speaking of Dave, we've got him right here. Our word was that the rescue has been a success. *(to the speaker:)* Dave? Can you hear me?

(The SOUND OF WIND, HELICOPTERS, WAVES, occasional SHOUTS, then DAVE'S voice, calm, collected.)

DAVE. Stanley! Congratulations! This is a great day for Mark & Maxwell, and I'm sure Maxolan-3000 will mark the start of a new era of strength for our company.

STAN. When do you expect to be back in the office, Dave?

DAVE. I'm currently on a rubber raft since the ship went under, but the helicopters are here, and I have every confidence I'll be back for the launch.

STAN. We look forward to seeing you, Dave.

DAVE. Incidentally, I can't say enough about my Executive Telephone — except for a few minor glitches it's really done the job. Looks like my ride is here.

(The sound of a HELICOPTER getting louder, then the SPEAKER goes dead.)

STAN. That's about it. As far as launch strategy, I've sketched out some changes for you to review by the end of the day. I believe Jeff is the only one who's seen them and I already have his input, but I look forward to reactions from the rest of you. Any questions you have will be dealt with at a general employees' meeting later this month. Thank you. *(DIANE, BEN and CARL Exit. STAN and ROXANNE are about to leave.)*

JEFF. Stan? Would it be possible for me to have a word with you?

STAN. *(quick glance at his watch)* Go ahead, Jeff.

JEFF. I mean in private.

STAN. Roxanne is going to be working very closely with me. Anything you say to me you're saying to her as well.

JEFF. I just wanted to apologize for punching you out. I hope that won't affect my future here. I didn't know...

STAN. I'll reassess all personnel at the end of the month.

JEFF. I know I haven't treated you very well. I'd like to change that. And I know I didn't give your launch plan the attention it deserves. I want to make it up to you.

STAN. That's not necessary. You'll continue in your

ACT II   **THE DOWNSIDE**   85

present position on an interim basis.

JEFF. Interim?

STAN. I'll be taking my cues from Roxanne on any changes in the Marketing Department. She knows how the office functions. *(STAN Exits.)*

JEFF. Roxanne, there's been a lot of kidding around with you and me...I hope you know how I meant it—

ROXANNE. I know exactly how you meant it, Jeff. *(ROXANNE Exits. JEFF is alone, then he leaves.)*

(DIANE re-enters the conference room. BEN Enters.)

BEN. Are you aware that I've been ignoring you?

DIANE. Yes, I am.

BEN. Good. I didn't want you to think I was just preoccupied or something.

DIANE. You came in here to tell me you're ignoring me?

BEN. Right. *(BEN turns to leave.)*

DIANE. Don't you think there are things more important than our feelings, Ben? Our company has been taken over. I don't know what to think. I don't know whether we've gained something or lost something. The only thing I do know is we've got a moral obligation to get Maxolan out there for the sake of the people who could benefit from it.

BEN. A moral obligation?

DIANE. I realize that isn't a word that comes up very often in here. But I think in this case it applies.

BEN. It must be nice to be so sure.

DIANE. What are you talking about?

BEN. Nothing that isn't in the doctors' reports. *(BEN Exits to his office. He dials the phone.)*

BEN. Jack? I want seven grand on any game you got going tonight. The Nets? Great, what's the spread? I get seven points? I'm there. Right, I know you're only doing this because we have a history. I win, we're even, I lose, you and Vito and all your thugs can come after me. I really appreciate it, buddy. *(He hangs up the phone.)* Asshole.

(CROSS FADE to JEFF'S office, formerly ALAN'S office. JEFF is at the desk. DIANE Enters.)

DIANE. I'd like to see all the doctors' reports on Maxolan-3000.

JEFF. You have all the information you need for this launch, Diane. What's the problem?

DIANE. I don't think there is a problem in wanting more information.

JEFF. Have you been talking to anyone in particular about this?

DIANE. Jeff, I would just feel better if—

JEFF. You would feel better if I was out of this office and you were in it.

DIANE. So you won't let me see any of the reports.

JEFF. There's nothing to see. But you have a very inquisitive mind, and that's a big help in this business. You also have a reputation for honesty, directness, intelligence...I'm thinking you might be in line for a new position working more directly with sales. I happen to know there's an opening in Kansas City Missouri. You like the midwest, don't you? *(DIANE goes to the reception area, gets her coat and Exits outside.)*

(CROSS FADE to BEN'S office. Dusk. JEFF Enters.)

BEN. So what do you think? Are we gonna pull this one out of the fire?

JEFF. I told you I would bring you back on staff, Ben. And I came through this mine-field with full power to do that. But you stabbed me in the back.

BEN. What are you saying?

JEFF. You've got a real problem with loyalty, don't you?

BEN. Would you talk to me, Jeff?

JEFF. Diane is onto this thing. The report. You know that broad has a major problem with her conscience—

BEN. That can be a real liability in this business—

JEFF. So you've put me in a bad place. We both knew we had to contain that report and you go and tell the worst person possible.

BEN. Jeff—

JEFF. Don't lie to me, Ben. How else would she know? I can't take the risk of you trashing this launch. You gotta leave. I'm sorry.

BEN. I guess if this company fires me enough times I really will have to leave.

JEFF. You're not dealing with a tired old man this time. I know you got problems but there's just too much at stake. Too much money, too many jobs, too many lives.

BEN. You sanctimonious fuck. You and your wife and

kid and all these lives you suddenly care about. I know you, Jeff. Don't ever think I don't know you. You're gutless. And I can see right into your rotten soul.

JEFF. Ben! I'm doing this because it's my job and I have a responsibility to this company. You think I want to fire my best friend?

BEN. We were never friends, Jeff. We were just two people who worked together, that's all.

(CROSS FADE to the reception area. JEFF is leaving when DIANE Enters from outside with a bag of take-out food.)

JEFF. Working late?
DIANE. That's right. Goodnight, Jeff. *(JEFF Exits outside.)*

(CROSS FADE to BEN'S office. DIANE Enters with the take-out food.)

DIANE. You don't have to eat this. I got it for you anyway.
BEN. What is it?
DIANE. Take out Mexican.
BEN. Chico's? *(She hands him the bag.)* Thanks, Diane.
DIANE. Now what's the story with the doctors' reports?
BEN. Oh, you think I can be bought with burritos and refried beans.
DIANE. Every man has his price.
BEN. Mine just happens to be incredibly low.
DIANE. There's a problem, right?

BEN. That's right. The problem is, you go to Jeff, use my name, and I get fired. And hell, in my case, that's not just losing my job, it's losing my house, too.

DIANE. My God! Now Jeff has fired you? Ben, I'm so sorry. But I didn't use your name. I just wanted to know what was in that report. I mean if we're going to push Maxolan we have to know—

BEN. I don't care. I don't work here anymore.

DIANE. Tell me what's in the report, Ben.

BEN. Okay, there's one report that says Maxolan might have certain side-effects when used in conjunction with certain other drugs.

DIANE. What side effects?

BEN. Well...this one guy Ryan alludes to delusional behavior, temporary mental impairment—

DIANE. Who knows about this?

BEN. It should have gone to Research. Alan knew. Jeff knows. Maybe more.

DIANE. So other people knew? And didn't do anything? I feel sick, Ben. I believed in this. That it meant something, that it was capable of actually doing some good in the world. I really wanted to believe that everything I have invested in this job and all the sacrifices and all the loneliness had some point.

BEN. This is one product, Diane. Probably a good one.

DIANE. What has always kept me going is this feeling of trust, that it did mean something. That if you worked hard you'd get somewhere and even do some good in the world and if you were kind to other people they would be kind to you. And when you lose that wide-eyed feeling of trust, well, you see that it's all really pretty awful, isn't it?

BEN. I'm prob'ly not the best one to talk to about faith and optimism and justice—

DIANE. There are times when I wonder if I will always feel as totally alone as I do now.

BEN. *(He puts his arm around her.)* You're not alone, Diane—

DIANE. I wasn't talking about you.

BEN. Good.

DIANE. But you have been a real jerk.

BEN. That's right. I don't care who I kick on the way down.

DIANE. I could take your mood swings, your preoccupation, but when you actually started ignoring me—

BEN. I was ignoring you because you were ignoring me!

DIANE. I was ignoring you because I like you and I was trying to get you to notice me.

BEN. Well I noticed alright, I noticed you were — wait a second, you ignored me because you liked me? What is this, eighth grade?

DIANE. Okay, it was a mistake, I'm sorry. I told Roxanne I liked you. She said I should treat you like dirt.

BEN. Roxanne said that? Great advice. I told Roxanne I liked you. She said I should go out of my way to be nice to you.

DIANE. So here we are.

BEN. *(He kisses her.)* I guess it worked.

DIANE. What are we going to do?

BEN. *(pulling her close)* Well...it's been a while but I remember the basics.

DIANE. I mean about Maxolan.

BEN. You're not looking for moral guidance from me, are you?

DIANE. I trust you, Ben. I think you're the most decent man I know.

BEN. I'd say you need a whole new circle of friends.

DIANE. No I don't. I just need one good friend.

BEN. Me too.

DIANE. So what are we going to do?

BEN. Diane, you're really asking me to make a decision? You don't know how uncomfortable that makes me feel.

DIANE. Then we're even. Because I'm having to make a decision I should have made a long time ago.

BEN. What's that? *(She throws her arms around him and kisses him.)* Here, I'll do the dishes. *(BEN takes the remains of the take-out dinner and tosses it in the trash.)* Would you like to listen to a ballgame later on?

DIANE. Why?

BEN. Oh, I'm kind of interested in sports.

DIANE. How much did you bet on this one?

BEN. I bet it all — just like the company. My kneecaps, my face, my car, my unborn children—

DIANE. Sure, I'll listen to the game with you. Can we call it a date? Because I haven't had many dates lately.

BEN. Yeah, we'll call it a date.

DIANE. What do we do until out date starts?

BEN. I don't know. I'm sure we can figure something out.

(BEN kisses her. BLACKOUT. In the darkness we hear the radio BROADCAST of the game that BEN bet on. The Nets win in the final seconds. A moment of silence.)

BEN. Thank you God. *(Laughter from BEN and DIANE in the darkness.)*

(END OF ACT II, SCENE 2

Scene 3

The next morning. LIGHTS up on the reception area. CARL is at ROXANNE'S desk, answering the phone, taking messages, obviously out of his league.

CARL. *(on phone)* No...no, I'm afraid he's gone. No, not dead, at least not that I know of. Retired. Can I take a message?

(STAN and ROXANNE Enter.)

ROXANNE. *(glancing at her clip-board)* Carl, I want you to call about the limos, they should be here by now. Check with National Video to make sure they've cleared the transmissions to all locations. I understand there was a problem with Houston.
CARL. I'll get right on it.
ROXANNE. Where's the coffee?

CARL. I haven't had time—

ROXANNE. Well make time, would you? I shouldn't have to do this myself. *(ROXANNE makes the coffee.)*

STAN. Have we got information on Dave?

CARL. There was a message, let's see... *(Goes through papers on desk.)* Yes, here it is. He definitely...uh...I think *will* be here for the launch. It's hard to read...either will or won't.

STAN. So it's definite that he either will or won't be here.

CARL. Correct.

ROXANNE. That's a big help, Carl.

CARL. I think it's "will."

STAN. Get confirmation, Carl. We can't wait forever.

(JEFF Enters.)

JEFF. Stan! You look great! You too, Roxanne. *(They ignore him.)* Everybody ready for the big day?

ROXANNE. We're waiting for Dave. He'll be in our limo.

STAN. If he's coming.

ROXANNE. Carl, make sure.

(GARY Enters, dressed in loud, inappropriate clothes. He has a video cassette.)

ROXANNE. Gary, have we cleared up the problem with Houston?

GARY. I've just been at the studio. Everything is cracker-jack, I checked the link-ups, we're all plugged in, ready to roll out the big guns and let'em have it, bang bang bang. *(beat)* Jeff? Your ideas were fantastic. I took what you said and ran it through my own personal consciousness and came up with a whole new take on the material. I tightened it up, moved things around, condensed it, focused on the main points, and we've got ourselves a hot little film that's better than sex.

JEFF. How little, Gary?

GARY. Two minutes eleven seconds.

JEFF. Down from four hours?

GARY. The kick is, I didn't lose a thing. Less is more, babe. Get'em in, get'em out. Now, as long as all the speakers got my memo — *(turning on STAN)* Stanley. What color is that shirt?

STAN. What?

GARY. Your shirt.

STAN. It's white.

GARY. It's white. Very good. I love you but you make me crazy. I said in the memo, blue shirt. It's video, Stan. I say this for your benefit, because you're the one out there looking like a dick-head—

JEFF. Gary! For Chrissakes calm down, would you?

STAN. This is a chance to show people what we've got. A safe cure for stress. I don't think there's anything to worry about. *(beat)* Roxanne, see if you can reach Dave.

ROXANNE. Carl, if he isn't at home, try his car.

CARL. *(on phone)* Okay, thank you, thank you. *(hangs up)* Gary? I'm getting a lot of calls from the regional sales offices. They want to know exactly what time the teleconference is supposed to start.

GARY. What's wrong with these people? I made it clear the conference begins at two o'clock.

CARL. Two o'clock our time, right?

GARY. It's the same time for everybody, Carl. I'm trying to keep this simple.

CARL. The Kansas City office thinks the launch is two o'clock their time, the L.A. office thinks it's two o'clock their time—

GARY. That's right, it's two o'clock for everybody, I'm not going to play favorites and have different times for different people. It's a live show, for Chrissakes! That's the whole point.

JEFF. Play favorites! What are you talking about, Gary?

ROXANNE. I think what Carl is trying to say is, those cities are in different time zones.

JEFF. Their two o'clock is different from our two o'clock.

STAN. Gary, if the L.A. sales team shows up at their regional sales meeting at two o'clock their time, they will be looking at a blank screen. Do you understand time zones, Gary?

GARY. Don't insult me, Stan. Not today. I've been up for a week, without sleep. If I have made a mistake with this time zone problem, whatever it is, I am sorry and I will fix it. Now indulge me, Stanley, and change the shirt. *(GARY Exits.)*

STAN. Carl, you understand time zones, don't you?

CARL. Yes, I do.

STAN. Good. I want you to go to central switchboard and get in touch with all the affiliates and straighten this out. Make sure they know the conference is two o'clock our time.

CARL. Right.

(CARL Exits. ALAN Enters with a bottle of champagne. He's wearing loud golf pants and a sports shirt.)

ALAN. Morning everybody! Just wanted to wish you all good luck!

ROXANNE. You look great, Alan. Retirement must be agreeing with you.

ALAN. Oh, I love it. Just love it. Now I've got a chance to do all the things I never had time for. *(turning on JEFF)* So...the big moment has finally arrived. Looks like you've got everything under control.

JEFF. We're in good shape, Alan.

ALAN. Good, good. Knew you would be. I guess I'll just hold onto this bottle 'til later. Or I could leave it if you don't want me around.

STAN. No, it's okay, Alan. We're going into the city in just a few minutes anyway.

ROXANNE. Just as soon as Dave shows up.

(CARL Enters.)

CARL. Alan! Good to see you!

ALAN. Hello, Carl.

CARL. So, what brings you back—

ROXANNE. What's the story, Carl? Are they taking care of this?

CARL. Everything's under control. *(beat)* Oh, I almost

forgot. It turns out Dave got back safely but he's tied up in meetings all day—

STAN. He won't be at the teleconference?

CARL. He wanted to have a word with everyone in the conference room. I'll call him right now.

(Everyone starts for the conference room, leaving ALAN alone in the reception area. BEN and DIANE Enter from outside.)

BEN. Alan!

ALAN. Hello, Ben. Diane.

DIANE. You look good, Alan.

ALAN. Thanks. You too.

DIANE. I don't know about that. But I sure feel good.

(CROSS FADE to the conference room. JEFF, STAN and ROXANNE are at the table. CARL is on the phone. ALAN Enters and stands off to the side. Then BEN and DIANE Enter.)

JEFF. Get the hell out of here, Ben.

DIANE. He's with me, Jeff. My guest. He can stay.

STAN. I thought he was fired.

JEFF. You can't sit at the table, Ben.

DIANE. For God's sakes, Jeff, it's his last day.

BEN. Don't worry, Jeff. I won't be going to the teleconference. I'll just stand over here with Alan. *(BEN moves over to ALAN.)* Anybody catch the Nets game last night?

CARL. *(stopping to talk)* Wasn't it something? I just saw the fourth quarter, when they kept coming back and coming back.

BEN. Three words for that game, Carl. Un-be-lievable.

STAN. Carl! Set up the speaker! You're keeping Dave waiting!

ROXANNE. *(to DIANE:)* Did you get all the learning systems out last night?

DIANE. No, I didn't. None of them went out last night.

ROXANNE. None of them? Why not?

DIANE. I was busy.

ROXANNE. I thought I had your personal assurance they'd be done—

(DAVE'S voice from the speaker.)

DAVE. —and in conclusion, I'd just like to say that I am as proud of this group as I can be—

CARL. Dave? Is that you?

DAVE. Of course it's me! Haven't you been listening?

CARL. We just got you on the speaker.

DAVE. I've been talking for five minutes. You didn't hear any of it?

STAN. I'm sorry about this, David. With the turn-over in this office we've had to help each other out—

DAVE. Forget it. I just want to wish you the best of luck. I'm sorry I can't actually be there in person, but I'll certainly be there in spirit. This is a tremendous moment in our company's history and it kicks off a whole new—

DIANE. Dave? I'm sorry to interrupt but I thought I should tell you. We have a problem—

JEFF. Diane!

DAVE. We don't have a lot of time. You can take this up

with Stan on your way into the city.

DIANE. But Dave, it's a problem that affects this launch.

JEFF. Diane!

DAVE. Look, I know this has been a tough deadline, we've all been under a lot of strain. But the bottom line is, we have a terrific product—

BEN. Dave?

DAVE. What is it, Jeff?

BEN. It's Ben—

DAVE. What's he doing there?

STAN. Ben, I'm going to have to ask you to leave—

JEFF. Don't listen to him, Dave. I already fired him.

BEN. Dave, what Diane is talking about is the product. There's a doctor's report that casts significant doubts on the safety of Maxolan.

DAVE. Ben, there's no problem. We already have FDA approval.

DIANE. That's the problem, Dave. This report wasn't sent to them. It claims that under certain conditions there could be temporary mental impairment, delusions — *(silence)*

DAVE. We'll have to look into this.

STAN. Why wasn't I sent a copy of this report?

BEN. We notified them last night of possible problems. They're expecting to hear from you today.

DAVE. This means a temporary hold on approval. Are you aware of what you've done?

DIANE. It was a matter of conscience, Dave.

ALAN. Dave? It's Alan—

JEFF. Shut up, Alan.

DAVE. What are you doing there, Alan? Is this an open house?

ALAN. Dave, I'm here because my heart is still with Mark & Maxwell. And I want to address what Ben and Diane have said. I saw that report months ago. I didn't think the results were valid. I knew it would cripple this company if we pulled Maxalon, so I told no one about it. To prove that it was a risk-free drug, I started taking Maxolan myself from the samples we had. There is no downside to this product, believe me. It helped me through the grief of losing my wife. It sharpened my mind because it allowed me to relax. It enabled me to see things I had never seen before. I was able to see relationships involved in world problems, and it allowed me to act on these problems. I made telephone calls, and before long, various world leaders whom I am not at liberty to name, started showing up at my home late at night. We discussed the issues while sitting at my kitchen table. Sometimes we drove around for hours, trying to find solutions. I believe I have done a damn good job in keeping the world in order, Dave, and I credit Maxolan for that. This drug must be distributed widely throughout this country and the world, because it has the power to transform our society, to remake our entire civilization, to make us the finest people we can be. Don't let anything stop you from this, Dave. *(silence)*

DAVE. Stan. In my office, immediately.

(STAN and ROXANNE leave. We hear the PHONE ringing in the reception area.)

ACT II **THE DOWNSIDE** 101

STAN. Get on that, Carl. *(CARL Exits.)*

ALAN. I hope to God you can get this thing back on track. I'd love to stay around and help, but Nixon's in my car and he hates to be kept waiting. *(ALAN and DIANE Exit. BEN and JEFF are alone.)*

JEFF. You had to bring everyone down with you, is that it?

BEN. Just once in my life I wanted to do the right thing.

JEFF. You think that was the right thing?

BEN. I don't know, Jeff. I just know how I feel right now.

JEFF. You're through, Ben. Not just here. Everywhere.

BEN. I know that, Jeff. And I'm leaving on my own. Get Maxolan out there, we can all spend our evenings meeting with world leaders.

JEFF. I'm doing my best, Ben.

BEN. I know you are, Jeff. That's the sad part.

(BEN Exits. CARL Enters.)

CARL. Jeff? Dave wants to talk to you, shall I put him through?

JEFF. Fine.

CARL. Also, Stan needs all your invoices on the teleconference. You can get that to me by the end of the day.

(CARL Exits. JEFF is sitting alone at the conference table. DAVE'S voice comes on the speaker.)

DAVE. Jeff?

JEFF. I'm listening, Dave.

DAVE. I want a full accounting of what we've spent on this launch. I want to know where every penny went. We're going to cut our losses and move forward.

JEFF. Sure, Dave.

DAVE. It's going to be an uphill battle, but with the merger we might do it. And Jeff? I just want you to know that your position with this company is secure. When Stanley moves on, there might be a place for you in corporate.

JEFF. Thanks, Dave.

DAVE. I want Ben out of the building.

JEFF. He's gone.

DAVE. Good. I'm going to put legal on this, see if we can stick the bastard with something. Any ideas you have would be welcome, you knew him pretty well, as I recall.

JEFF. Ben? I thought I did. We used to get together socially sometimes, but that kind of tapered off, you know? Something happened. I don't know what the hell it was. I don't understand what he thought he was doing. I thought we were on the same team. I thought we were friends. Jesus Christ, Dave, I don't know why he did that to us. I'm not sure I know anything anymore. *(beat)* I'd like to discuss this with you. See, there really isn't anyone for me to talk to around here any more. Dave? Can we get together and touch base on this, the two of us?

(We hear the DIAL TONE from the speaker. The LIGHTS hold on JEFF and come up on the reception area. ROXANNE is there,

clip-board in hand. DIANE Enters.)

DIANE. Who should I give my letter of resignation to?

ROXANNE. I'll take it.

DIANE. *(Hands her the letter.)* Roxanne, I want to thank you for what happened with Ben—

ROXANNE. I really don't have time. Is this decision final?

DIANE. Yes, it is.

(DIANE leaves. The LIGHTS hold on JEFF at the conference table, ROXANNE in the reception area, and come up on BEN'S office. BEN is packing his things. DIANE Enters with her coat on. She stands in the doorway. There's an awkwardness between them.)

DIANE. I just wanted to wish you well, Ben.

BEN. Thanks. I hope I can see you sometime. Even though I don't work here anymore.

DIANE. Oh, well, I don't work here anymore either.

BEN. They cancelled the launch. You could stay on.

DIANE. I already turned in my letter of resignation.

BEN. Not 'cause of me, I hope.

DIANE. You just made it easier.

BEN. *(picking up his things)* Are you leaving right now? 'Cause I could walk you out—

DIANE. No reason to stick around. *(beat)* Do you have a place to stay? *(They are now close together.)*

BEN. Not exactly. Something will turn up.

DIANE. Because there's an extra bedroom in my apartment. I mean if you wanted to stay, just temporarily—

BEN. Sorry, Diane. I couldn't do that.

DIANE. No, that's okay, I just thought if you needed a place—

BEN. I don't want to stay in the extra bedroom, Diane. *(They smile at each other.)*

DIANE. Oh, well, that would be fine too.

(BEN and DIANE Exit to the reception area. CARL is at the reception desk. BEN hands him the briefcase from the Christmas party. Then BEN and DIANE leave. We see Jeff in the conference room, CARL clutching the breifcase and ROXANNE in the reception area, rigid, on the phone. BLACKOUT.)

THE END

SOUND LIST

There is the possibility of a speaker and mike in a phone unit.
Speaker for Dave in Conference Room with switch on top and long cord.
Intercom speaker in Conference Room.
Tape player in Conference Room.
Monitor or headsets for Dave's location.

Music top of show
Airport ambience
"Flight to..." announcement
Dial tone
Music end of I-1
Party ambience
Dial tone
Christmas carols
Jet noise
Hijacking
Gunshot
Scene change music I-2 into I-3
Music end of I-3
Music top of Act II
Hostage
Gunshot
Dial tone
Music II-1 into II-2
Helicopters

Helicopter arriving
Dial tone
Basketball game
Dial tone
Music end of play

PRELIMINARY PROP LIST

ONSTAGE PRESET:
RECEPTION OFFICE U.S.:
Reception desk with:
> Master switchboard phone
> Message pad
> Pens/pencils
> Computer terminal on table UC
> Typewriter
> Desk lamp

Chair
Sofa with end table
End table:
> Coffee maker (on top)
> Coffee
> Mugs or cups
> Packets of coffee to be made
> Coffee stirs
> Sugar and cream packets
> Extra pots for scene changes

Additional supplies:
> Yellow pads
> Pencils
> Stapler (Roxanne staples memo to bulletin board)
> Memo pads

Message stand with office memos and information
Planter (4'-5')

Counter with Xerox machine C.L. in hallway
    Paper on shelf

ALAN'S OFFICE:
Desk with:
    Desk light
    Phone
    Papers and folders
    Pencils/pens
    Pills in desk drawer which locks (key)
Desk chair (high back)
2 chairs
File cabinet with lots of papers and files which get pulled out during I-3 when the Maxolan report is found.
Wastebasket
3-4 planters
Cart with TV/VCR

BEN'S OFFICE:
Desk with:
    Phone
    Papers/files
    Pencils/pens
    Desk lamp
Desk chair
Loveseat used as bed for Ben to sleep on.
    Cushions removable
Armchair
Wastebasket

THE DOWNSIDE

JEFF'S OFFICE:
Desk with:
- Phone
- Pens/pencils
- Papers/folders
- (Jeff and Stan have a fight which involves Stan falling over and behind the desk.)
- Desk light

Desk chair
Arm chair
Guest chair
Dictaphone
Wastebasket

CONFERENCE ROOM:
8 chairs
Console with:
- Phone
- Speaker for Dave (Long wire so it can be moved to the head of the table.)
- Tape player
- Ashtrays

PROPS

ACT I SCENE 1
Briefcase (Diane)
Briefcase (Ben)
Briefcase (Carl)
Briefcase (Jeff) (Papers taken out in II-2)
Briefcase (Alan)
Aspirin (Diane)
Knapsack (Carl)

ACT I SCENE 2
Garland around table in Conference Room
"Merry Christmas" sign strung in Reception
Box of Christmas decorations (Roxanne) (The Conference Room gets decorated.)
"Farewell Carl" sign which gets strung in Conference Room
Punch bowl with punch and glasses (Conference Room)
Little artificial Christmas tree with blinking lights (Conference Room)
Mouthwash (Ben)
Newspaper (Ben)
Ben's office gets cluttered with personal things ie:
    Clothes
    Suitcase
Stan's outline of Launch
Diane has lots of paperwork
Legal pads get set on conference table (Roxanne)

THE DOWNSIDE 111

Paper sack with:
> Roast beef on rye with lettuce, tomato, mayo
> Coke
> Bag of chips

Home camera

Video camera (Gary) (Batteries are changed onstage.) (Hooks up to equipment and used onstage with video screens.)

Belt pack

Jeff messes up his office during a tantrum.

Tape player with Christmas Carols playing in Conference Room

Colorfully wrapped present which is opened each performance only to reveal another briefcase

Joint and lighter (Gary)

ACT I SCENE 3

Conference Room has been cleaned up during scene change.

Ben's office in shambles—he is living there. I.e.:
> Blanket
> Newspapers
> Clothes
> Cushions or pillows

In Reception:
> Danishes on counter
> Full coffee pot
> Straws

Whiskey bottle—pint (Ben)

ACT II SCENE 1

Roxanne is collating papers

Ben enters from his office with a pile of papers he was collating for Roxanne.
Copies of Maxolan Report
Roxanne is setting up for a meeting in Conf. Room:
    More yellow pads
    Pencils
Potato chips (Gary)
Alan cleans out his desk:
    Personal office supplies
    Box

ACT II SCENE 2
Memo which Roxanne staples to the bulletin board
Video cassette (Gary)
Real estate ads from newspaper (Ben)
Notebook and pen (Gary)
2nd pint of whiskey (Ben)
Bag of take-out food (Diane) (Food is eaten onstage and containers are thrown away.)
Plastic forks
Napkins

ACT II SCENE 3
Clipboard (Roxanne)
Coffee is made onstage (3rd coffee pot?)
2nd video cassette
Letter of resignation (Diane)
Ben is packing his things up.
Bottle of Champagne—unopened (Alan)
Shrubs with snow along window line
2 bare trees